THE SERIAL KILLER

COOKBOOK

True Crime Trivia and Disturbingly Delicious Last Meals from Death Row's Most Infamous Killers and Murderers

Ashley Lecker

ULYSSES PRESS

Published by:
ULYSSES PRESS
P.O. Box 3440
Berkeley, CA 94703
www.ulyssespress.com

ISBN: 978-1-64604-023-0
Library of Congress Control Number: 2019951403

Printed in the United States by Versa Press
10 9 8 7 6 5 4

Acquisitions editor: Claire Sielaff
Managing editor: Claire Chun
Editor: Lauren Harrison
Proofreader: Barbara Schultz
Production: what!design @ whatweb.com
Cover artwork: photograph © Ashley Lecker; cleaver © shutterstock.com/GeorgeJ
Interior photographs: © Ashley Lecker
Interior illustrations: all from shutterstock.com—cleaver throughout © GeorgeJ;
    page 10 © Pinchuk Oleskandra; pages 16, 35, and 77 © VectorSun; page 18
    © Victoria Sergeeva; page 20 © Olga_Zaripova; page 27 © freelanceartist;
    page 45 © Fischer Fotostudio; page 47 © SpicyTruffel; page 50 © Yevheniia
    Lytvynovych; page 51 © Natalya Levish; page 56 © Victoria Sergeeva and
    © Bodor Tivadar; page 72 © Katrinaku; page 76 © father; page 84 © Actor
    and © MaKars; page 110 © AVA Bitter; page 111 © Siberian Art; page 114
    © Kate Macate and © SpicyTruffel; page 115 © Yevgen Kravchenko

For my boys

CONTENTS

INTRODUCTION

Welcome to one of the most morbidly themed cookbooks out there today! But let's face it: If you've picked this book up, you already get it. You've probably been fascinated or at least intrigued by true crime since a young age. You like interesting facts and spooky stories. You like listening to podcasts and watching documentaries about cold cases, infamous crimes, and the people that committed them. So why not bring that passion of yours into the kitchen?

A BIT ABOUT LAST MEALS

In many countries, the last meal is a customary allowance granted to death row prisoners before their executions. Of course, the requests must be within reason, and tobacco, beer, wine, and liquor are usually denied nowadays. If the inmate's request is too outlandish, the prison will usually provide them with a substitute, or the meal being served in the cafeteria at that time. There are other restrictions too. For example, in Florida, the meal's total cost must be under $40, and the ingredients must be available locally. That means no one is flying out to Russia for caviar!

Texas no longer allows the ritual of last meals at all, thanks to the prisoner Lawrence Russell Brewer (we'll learn about him later), who refused to eat the massive amount of food he'd requested, claiming he wasn't actually hungry. Now those on death row in Texas detention centers receive the same meal as everyone else on their last day.

A BIT ABOUT THIS COOKBOOK

You'll find that this cookbook isn't organized like most others, with appetizers first and desserts last. Instead, *The Serial Killer Cookbook* is organized alphabetically by the names of death row inmates. After all, this is a book of last meal recipes. In each inmate's section, you'll find a home-cooked version of at least one of their last meal components. Some of them got greedy (who actually needs two liters of Pepsi, or two pitchers of milk?), so I've selected the best parts of each meal and put my own spin on the recipe so the results will taste less like prison food and more like a delicious, home-made dish. Some of these men were determined to make their last meals as creepy as possible (a single black, unpitted olive? seriously?), and so I've taken the liberty of turning those requests into tastier versions of the originals. In the accompanying photos, I've styled these dishes on prison-applicable trays, bowls, and plates, but trust me—these meals will taste just as good on your regular old dishware! No plastic sporks necessary.

Since many last meals featured repeating elements like fried chicken, I've added suggestions for recipe pairings in the notes of each inmate's section, so you can compile your own meals from the recipes in this book.

A BIT ABOUT THE TRIVIA

Since this is a cookbook about murderers on death row, we're walking a fine line between fascinating and downright disgusting. Each entry has a note summarizing the killer's life and bad deeds, but I haven't gone into the gory details. After all, I wouldn't want to ruin your appetite!

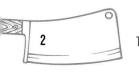

LAST MEAL

RECIPES

STEPHEN WAYNE ANDERSON July 8, 1953–January 29, 2002

Stephen Wayne Anderson was an American murderer—specifically a contract killer. In 1979, Anderson escaped from prison in Utah, where he was incarcerated for aggravated burglary, and went on to undertake contract killings and work with drug traffickers. Anderson was arrested again after he murdered 81-year-old Elizabeth Lyman in her home. After Anderson killed Lyman, he looked for money (but found little), and made himself a meal in her kitchen. Since most 81-year-old ladies aren't up cooking meals at midnight, the unusual late-night activity alerted neighbors who called the cops. Upon his arrest, Anderson admitted to at least six contract killings, but he was responsible for a total of nine known murders. In 2002, Anderson was executed by lethal injection at San Quentin State Prison in California.

LAST MEAL: two grilled cheese sandwiches, one pint of cottage cheese, a hominy-corn mixture, radishes, one piece of peach pie, and one pint of chocolate chip ice cream.

GRILLED CHEESE

Out of Anderson's dairy-heavy meal, I've chosen to focus on a recipe for the ultimate grilled cheese. This recipe follows a traditional route with three slices of American cheese, but feel free to add your own favorites like Gouda or cheddar. And don't be afraid to make it a double like Anderson did.

MAKES: 1 serving | **PREP TIME:** 3 minutes | **COOK TIME:** 8 to 9 minutes

INGREDIENTS
2 slices sourdough bread
1½ tablespoons salted butter
3 slices American cheese

1. Heat a griddle to medium-low heat. Ensure that the griddle or pan is not too hot, because you want the bread to toast, not burn.

2. Spread the butter on one side of each piece of bread. Place one slice on the griddle and add the cheese. Place the second on top.

3. Allow the sandwich to cook for about 5 minutes, until the first side is toasted and golden. Check to make sure it is cooked, then flip. Typically, the second side cooks a little faster and will only need 3 to 4 minutes, so keep an eye on it!

4. Remove from the griddle, cut in half, and serve.

JOE ARRIDY ✂ April 29, 1915–January 6, 1939

Joe Arridy was an American from Colorado who was falsely accused, convicted, and executed for murder of a 15-year-old girl. Arridy suffered from mental illness and had a low IQ, and though he admitted to the murder, it is believed that Arridy's confession was a false one. Arridy was executed in the gas chamber in 1939.

LAST MEAL: ice cream.

NO-CHURN VANILLA ICE CREAM

In line with Arridy's simple request, this is a recipe for an easy, creamy vanilla ice cream. Though it may seem like a hassle to make your own ice cream at home, it actually isn't too tedious. And trust me — the results are worth it!

MAKES: 4 servings | **PREP TIME:** 15 minutes | **FREEZER TIME:** 12 hours

INGREDIENTS

2 cups heavy cream

1 (14-ounce) can sweetened condensed milk

1½ teaspoons vanilla extract

1. In a stand mixer with the whisk attachment, whip the heavy cream on high until stiff peaks form, 2 to 3 minutes.

2. In a medium bowl, stir together the condensed milk and vanilla. Gently fold the whipped cream into the condensed milk mixture.

3. Pour the cream mixture into a 9 x 5-inch loaf pan. Make sure the mixture is sitting evenly in the pan. Cover tightly. Freeze at least 12 hours before serving. Best served no more than 30 to 45 days after the first freezing.

ODELL BARNES

March 22, 1968–March 1, 2000

Odell Barnes, Jr. was an American from Texas charged with the 1989 murder of 42-year-old Helen Bass, and was convicted and sentenced in very quick succession. The fast progress of the trial, jury conviction, and death sentence attracted the attention of anti-death penalty groups, as well as international criticism. Despite the uproar, Barnes was executed in 2000 by lethal injection.

LAST MEAL: "Justice, equality, world peace."

EASY HOMEMADE DINNER ROLLS

As a home cook, one could interpret Barnes's unique request as pretty much anything, but I've gone with a simple and satisfying classic: bread. While these rolls are delicious on their own (especially fresh out of the oven), I've paired them with a tasty lemon and olive oil-infused butter.

MAKES: 12 Rolls | **PREP:** 45 minutes | **COOK TIME:** 20 minutes

INGREDIENTS

2 cups all-purpose flour, divided

1 (.25-ounce) package active dry yeast

2 tablespoons granulated sugar

½ teaspoon salt

½ cup whole milk

¼ cup water

2 tablespoons melted butter

1. Add ¾ cup flour, yeast, sugar, and salt to a large bowl. In a small saucepan, heat the milk, water, and butter until steaming, and just under a simmer. Add to the flour mixture. Using an electric mixer, beat at medium speed for 2 minutes, scraping the bowl as needed. Add ¼ cup flour and beat 1 minute at high speed. Stir in the remaining 1 cup of flour—the dough should be soft.

2. Knead the dough on a floured surface until smooth, about 8 minutes. Cover and let the dough rest for 10 minutes on the counter.

3. Divide the dough into 12 equal pieces and shape into balls. Place in a greased 8-inch round pan. Cover and allow the dough to rise until it has doubled in size, 25 to 30 minutes.

4. Preheat the oven to 375°F and bake for 20 minutes. Remove from the oven and brush with butter. Serve warm or at room temperature.

THE SERIAL KILLER COOKBOOK

LEMON AND OLIVE OIL-INFUSED BUTTER

To go with the Easy Homemade Dinner Rolls (page 8), try this elevated take on butter. The addition of olive oil in the recipe is inspired by the olive branch, a well-known symbol of peace. See what I did there?

MAKES: ½ cup infused butter | **PREP TIME:** 5 minutes

INGREDIENTS

½ cup salted butter (1 stick), softened

1 teaspoon fresh lemon zest

1 teaspoon olive oil

¼ teaspoon fresh cracked pepper

In a small bowl with a lid, stir together the butter, lemon zest, olive oil, and pepper. Cover and refrigerate for about 10 minutes to allow the butter to set, but still be soft. Serve with bread. The butter can be kept at room temperature for 7 to 10 hours or stored in the fridge for up to 30 days.

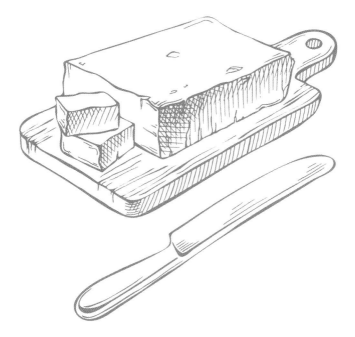

WILLIAM BONIN January 8, 1947–February 23, 1996

William Bonin was an American serial killer and sex offender also known as the Freeway Killer. In his first trial, the prosecutor dubbed him "the most arch-evil person who ever existed," and this was pretty spot-on. Bonin was convicted of 14 counts of murder, but was likely responsible for more than 36. Like many serial offenders, Bonin grew up in an extremely abusive home and began committing petty crimes at a young age. During his teenage years, Bonin began to molest victims who were younger than him. These acts would continue to escalate as he grew older.

As a young adult, Bonin joined the Air Force and served in the Vietnam War. The things he experienced during active duty made him come to believe that human life was overvalued. In the late 1960s, Bonin was arrested for physically and sexually assaulting young boys and was institutionalized before being relocated to prison because he kept sexually assaulting fellow patients. For some incomprehensible reason, Bonin was deemed no longer a danger to others, and he was released from prison in 1974. Shortly after his release he assaulted another boy, was arrested *again* and sent to prison *again*, though this sentence would last only three years.

The majority of Bonin's crimes occurred in 1979–80 along the highways of California, earning him the "Freeway Killer" title. He would lure victims into his Ford Econoline van, which he had rigged so that victims could not easily escape, before sexually assaulting and murdering them.

During this spree, Bonin had several accomplices. He was often accompanied by 21-year-old Vernon Butts or 18-year-old Gregory Miley. 17-year-old William Ray Pugh also accompanied Bonin, and would eventually tip off the police to Bonin's activities.

After a period of police surveillance (thanks in part to Pugh's tip), Bonin was arrested while in the middle of committing another assault. In 1982, he was convicted of 10 murders and sentenced to death. In 1983, Bonin was convicted of an additional four murders in Orange County, California, and given the death penalty. After numerous appeals, in 1996, Bonin was executed in California by lethal injection.

LAST MEAL: two pepperoni and sausage pizzas, three servings of chocolate ice cream, and three six-packs of Coca-Cola and Pepsi. He shared his feast with five others. Generous, sure, but that doesn't make him any less of a terrible person!

NO-CHURN CHOCOLATE ICE CREAM

Taken from Bonin's meal, here is a recipe for an easy no-churn chocolate ice cream. If you'd like to make this recipe even more chocolaty, try adding chocolate chunks or a fudge swirl to step 3!

MAKES: 4 servings | **PREP TIME:** 15 minutes | **FREEZER TIME:** 12 hours

INGREDIENTS

2 cups heavy cream

1 (14-ounce) can sweetened condensed milk

½ teaspoon vanilla extract

2 tablespoons unsweetened cocoa powder

½ cup chocolate chunks or ⅓ cup jarred chocolate fudge (optional)

1. In a stand mixer with the whisk attachment, whip the heavy cream on high speed until stiff peaks form, 2 to 3 minutes.

2. In a medium bowl, stir together the condensed milk, cocoa powder, and vanilla. Gently fold the whipped cream into the condensed milk mixture.

3. Pour the cream mixture into a 9 x 5-inch loaf pan. If you choose to add chocolate chunks or a fudge swirl, stir them into the cream mixture now. Make sure the cream is sitting evenly in the pan. Cover tightly. Freeze at least 12 hours before serving. Best served no more than 30 to 45 days after the first freezing.

THE SERIAL KILLER COOKBOOK

LAWRENCE RUSSELL BREWER  March 13, 1967–September 21, 2011

Lawrence Russell Brewer was an American murderer and white supremacist from Texas. He and two accomplices were responsible for the torture and murder of an African-American man named James Byrd, Jr., in 1998. Brewer and his friends offered Byrd a ride and brought him to a remote area where they beat him. After, Byrd was tied to the back of the truck and dragged about three miles to his death, and the men then dumped his body in front of a cemetery. Brewer and his friends went to a barbecue, and Byrd was not discovered until the next morning.

Byrd's murder inspired the passing of the James Byrd Jr. Hate Crimes Act in 2001, and, along with the murder of Matthew Shepard, the Matthew Shepard and James Byrd Jr. Hate Crimes Prevention Act in 2009.

Brewer was sentenced to death and was executed for his crime (for which he never showed remorse) in 2011 by lethal injection.

LAST MEAL: two chicken-fried steaks with gravy and sliced onions; a triple-meat bacon cheeseburger with fixings on the side; a cheese omelet with ground beef, tomatoes, onions, bell peppers, and jalapeños; fried okra with ketchup; one pound of barbecue with half a loaf of white bread; three fajitas with fixings; a Meat Lover's pizza (typically pepperoni, sausage, bacon, Canadian bacon, and ground beef); three root beers; one pint of Blue Bell vanilla ice cream; and a slab of peanut butter fudge with crushed peanuts. Brewer then refused the meal he'd requested, after which Texas stopped offering last meals statewide.

CHICKEN-FRIED STEAK WITH GRAVY AND ONIONS

This recipe serves as a representative from Brewer's excessive and entitled order.

MAKES: 2 to 4 servings | **PREP TIME:** 15 minutes | **COOK TIME:** 15 minutes

FOR THE STEAK:

1 pound round cube steaks (about 4 small or 2 large steaks)

1 teaspoon salt, plus ½ teaspoon for seasoning

1 teaspoon pepper, plus ¼ teaspoon for seasoning

½ cup all-purpose flour

1 teaspoon cornstarch

¼ teaspoon onion powder

¼ teaspoon garlic powder

2 eggs

1 tablespoon water

1 cup vegetable oil

FOR THE GRAVY:

¼ cup chopped white onion

2 cups beef broth

1½ tablespoons all-purpose flour

½ cup whole milk

1. To make the steak, remove the steaks from the fridge. Season on both sides with the salt and pepper. Allow to sit at room temperature for about 10 minutes so the steak will not be as cold and will not lower the oil temperature as greatly when it fries.

2. In a large shallow dish, mix the flour, cornstarch, garlic powder, onion powder, pepper, and salt. In a second large shallow dish, beat the eggs and water.

3. Set up an assembly line starting with the wet mixture, then the dry mixture, and a clean plate at the end.

4. Pour the oil into a large cast-iron skillet so it comes about 1 inch up the side. Heat over medium-high until an instant-read thermometer registers 350°F.

5. With your left hand, dip a steak into the egg mixture. Transfer to your right hand and dip it in the flour. Press the flour into the steak so it is evenly coated. Place the steak on the clean plate. Repeat with the remaining steaks. Keeping one hand dry will be helpful to reduce sticking and make the breading process more efficient.

6. Fry the steak a few pieces at a time, until golden brown and a thermometer inserted into the center reads 160°F, about 3 to 4 minutes on each side. Drain on paper towel–lined plates and loosely cover with foil to help the steak stay warm while gravy is prepared.

7. To make the gravy, pour most of the oil from the out of the pan. Add the onions and cook for 1 minute. In a small bowl, whisk together the broth, flour, and milk. Add to the skillet and bring to a simmer to allow the gravy to thicken, about 3 minutes. Make sure to stir to prevent burning.

8. Serve the steaks with gravy poured over the top.

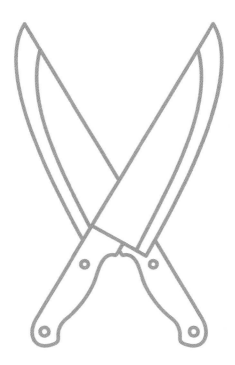

THE SERIAL KILLER COOKBOOK

ROBERT ANTHONY BUELL  September 10, 1940–September 24, 2002

Robert Anthony Buell was a child murderer from Ohio. He was convicted of killing Krista Lea Harrison after abducting her while she was cleaning up a park with a friend only 300 feet away from her home. The case went unsolved for over a year before Buell became a suspect. Fibers from his van, plastic packaging, and paint from his home matched materials found on Harrison's body. Buell disputed the charges but was found guilty and sentenced to death.

Buell was also suspected, but not convicted, of the murders of 12-year-old Tina Marie Harmon in 1981 and 10-year-old Debora Kaye Smith in 1983. He was executed by lethal injection in Ohio in 2002. For his last meal, Buell underscored his inherent creepiness by requesting a single pitted olive.

LAST MEAL: a single unpitted olive.

SINGLE-OLIVE TAPENADE

Since it's quite easy to pull an olive out of a jar and put it on a plate, I've interpreted Buell's request a little differently. This tapenade uses pitted green olives, capers, garlic, pimentos, lemon juice, and olive oil. Serve it on toast or spread on a sandwich.

MAKES: 1 cup | **PREP TIME:** 5 minutes

INGREDIENTS

2 cups pitted green olives

1 tablespoon capers

2 cloves garlic

1 tablespoon pimentos

¼ teaspoon pepper

1 teaspoon lemon juice

¼ cup olive oil

toast or crusty bread, for serving

1. Place all the ingredients into a food processor and pulse until roughly chopped.

2. Remove and serve with toast or bread.

Ted Bundy is potentially one of the most well-known and documented serial killers in the United States. Bundy was born in 1946 in Vermont at a home for single mothers. He was raised by his grandparents and was told that his mother was actually his older sister. He eventually found out the truth, after which his mother married a new man named Johnny Bundy.

During high school, Bundy engaged in a few thefts, which were expunged from his record when he turned 18. It is not clear when Bundy began killing; some estimate it was the early 1970s, others think mid- to late-1960s, and some theorize it started when he was a teenager. However, it is certain that while he lived in Washington state, many women began to go missing. It is reported that he would occasionally wear an arm sling when luring his victims, asking for help carrying a load of books to his tan Volkswagen Beetle.

A police sketch was put out of the man who was murdering women, and Bundy's girlfriend and coworkers reported the resemblance, but the police never followed up on due to the onslaught of tips and the fact that Bundy didn't seem like a stereotypical criminal. Bundy then moved to Utah to attend law school, where the disappearances continued. While there, Bundy was eventually arrested and charged with kidnapping and assault. He was later charged with murder in Colorado and acted as his own attorney, which helped facilitate his escape. After jumping out of a window in the law library, Bundy managed to elude capture for six days in the mountains before he was returned to custody. This was not Bundy's only escape. Before his trial in Colorado, Bundy managed to escape through the ceiling of his cell and made his way across the Midwest, Georgia, and Florida.

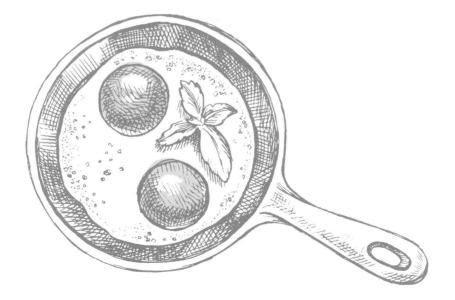

In 1978, early in the morning, Bundy entered the Florida State University Chi Omega sorority and brutally attacked four women; two survived. He remained in the area attacking and killing until he was arrested near the Florida–Alabama state line. He had court-appointed attorneys, but acted as his own counsel for a majority of the trial, and was ultimately convicted and sentenced to death by electric chair three different times. Bundy's execution was originally scheduled in 1986, but it was stayed as he began to confess to his crimes. Bundy went into detail about the places where he revisited his victims, such as Taylor Mountain, and would lie with the bodies or perform other sexual acts. He also confessed to burning a victim's head in a friend's fireplace. The victims were from different states, and the further details Bundy provided helped close cases and give closure to the victims' families. During this time Bundy was interviewed by the Washington police, who hoped that he could help shed light on the investigation of the Green River Killer. Bundy was executed by electric chair in Florida in 1989.

LAST MEAL: Bundy did not request a final meal, and was given steak, eggs, hash browns, toast with butter and jelly, milk, coffee, and juice. He did not eat any of it.

SEARED STEAK

This recipe is a seared steak made in a cast-iron pan served with fried eggs and toast. Searing a steak is key to the cooking process; it "seals in the juices" and allows for a deliciously textured crust on the outside of the steak, promoting incredible flavor.

MAKES: 1 serving | **PREP:** 15 minutes | **COOK:** 8 minutes

FOR THE STEAK:

1 (12-ounce) ribeye steak

½ teaspoon salt

½ teaspoon pepper

2 tablespoons unsalted butter

1 tablespoon olive oil

toast, for serving

FOR THE EGGS:

1 tablespoon salted butter

½ teaspoon vegetable oil

2 large eggs

salt and pepper

1. To make the steak, remove the steak from fridge. Allow the steak to come to room temperature on the counter for about 15 minutes. Pat dry and season liberally with salt and pepper.

2. Heat a 10 to 12-inch cast-iron skillet over medium-high. Add the butter and oil.

3. Add the steak to the hot skillet. It should loudly sizzle when it makes contact with the pan. Cook 3 to 4 minutes per side. Check the internal temperature of the steak and remove when it reaches 135°F. Allow steak to rest for about 2 minutes before serving.

4. To make the eggs, heat the butter and oil in a medium nonstick skillet over medium heat just before the steak is done cooking.

5. Break the eggs, one at a time, into the skillet, leaving room between them.

6. Cook 4 minutes, or until the whites are just set and the yolks are still runny. If you prefer a medium- to well-done yolk, cook for an additional minute or two. If desired, season eggs with salt and pepper.

7. Serve eggs alongside the steak, with toast on the side.

ALTON COLEMAN ✂ November 6, 1955–April 26, 2002

Alton Coleman was an American spree killer. Along with his accomplice, Debra Brown, he committed eight murders across multiple Midwestern states. Brown met Coleman shortly before the 1984 murders, and she left her family to be with him. Coleman was sentenced to death in three states. He was executed in Ohio in 2002.

LAST MEAL: well-done filet mignon with mushrooms, fried chicken breasts, salad with French dressing, sweet potato pie with whipped cream, French fries, collard greens, onion rings, cornbread, broccoli with melted cheese, biscuits and gravy, and a cherry Coke.

BISCUITS AND SAUSAGE GRAVY

Biscuits and gravy is a timeless dish that dates back to Jamestown. Nowadays, it's even easier to make thanks to premade biscuits and store-bought sausage!

MAKES: 6 servings | **PREP TIME:** 10 minutes | **COOK TIME:** 15 minutes

INGREDIENTS

1 (16-ounce) can refrigerated jumbo buttermilk biscuits

1 pound ground pork sausage

2 tablespoons unsalted butter

¼ cup all-purpose flour

2¾ cups whole milk

2 teaspoons pepper

¼ teaspoon salt

½ teaspoon garlic powder

1. Bake the biscuits according to the package instructions.

2. While the biscuits are cooking, brown the pork in a 10 to 12-inch cast-iron skillet until no longer pink, about 4 minutes. Add the butter to the skillet and allow it to melt.

3. Add the flour and stir to coat. Add the milk and gently stir to allow the gravy to thicken, 3 to 4 minutes. Add the pepper, salt, and garlic powder.

4. Split the biscuits in half and serve the gravy on top.

SERVE WITH: Seared Steak (page 22) and Crispy Fried Chicken (page 42)

GREEN ONION AND PEPPERCORN DROP BISCUITS

If you've got a little more time on your hands, I suggest making your biscuits from scratch. It's easier than you think, and the results are super delicious!

MAKES: 6 biscuits | **PREP TIME:** 10 minutes | **COOK TIME:** 12 minutes

INGREDIENTS

¾ cup all-purpose flour

1 teaspoon baking powder

¼ teaspoon baking soda

½ teaspoon salt

½ teaspoon black pepper

2 tablespoons cold unsalted butter, cut into small pieces

¼ cup minced green onion

⅓ cup plain Greek yogurt

1. Preheat the oven to 425°F. Line a baking sheet with parchment paper and set aside.

2. Sift the first 5 ingredients together in a medium bowl. Add the butter and mix with a fork until you have a mealy texture.

3. Gently stir in the green onion and yogurt. Mix just until the dough is soft and sticky dough just comes together.

4. Divide the dough into 6 portions and drop onto the prepared baking sheet. Bake for 12 to 14 minutes. The top will be a light golden brown.

FRANCIS CROWLEY  October 31, 1912–January 21, 1932

Francis Crowley, a quintessential 1930s gangster, went on a crime spree that ended in a two-hour shootout with the New York City Police Department. Crowley often carried two pistols and would simultaneously shoot them, earning him the nickname "Two Gun." His crime spree began in February 1931 when he crashed an American Legion dance and shot at two men when he was removed from the venue. The crimes escalated in the following months, and Crowley was eventually captured after a shootout with around 300 police officers and a whopping 15,000 spectators. The teenaged Crowley was a nuisance while incarcerated (he even set fire to his bed!), but calmed down toward the end and even kept a pet bird in his cell. He was executed in the electric chair at Sing Sing at age 19.

LAST MEAL: steak and onions, French fries, apple pie, and both ice cream and melted ice cream.

A BOWL OF MELTED ICE CREAM

This recipe is a bowl of melted vanilla ice cream adorned with a few black sprinkles for Crowley's crimes. Melted ice cream is more delicious than you might think! It is also a popular ingredient for cakes and results in moist and flavorful baked goodies.

MAKES: 4 servings | **PREP TIME:** 15 minutes | **FREEZER TIME:** 12 hours | **COOK TIME:** 30 seconds

INGREDIENTS

2 cups heavy cream

1 (14-ounce) can sweetened condensed milk

½ teaspoon vanilla extract

sprinkles, for serving (optional)

1. In a stand mixer with the whisk attachment, whip the heavy cream on high until stiff peaks form, about 2 to 3 minutes.

2. Stir the condensed milk and vanilla in a medium bowl. Gently fold the whipped cream into the mixture.

3. Pour the cream mixture into a 9 x 5-inch loaf pan. Make sure the cream is sitting evenly in the pan. Cover tightly. Freeze at least 12 hours before serving. Best served no more than 30 to 45 days after the first freezing.

4. To melt the ice cream, place a few scoops in a microwave-safe bowl and cook until soft. Stir until smooth and liquid. Top with sprinkles.

SERVE WITH: Seared Steak (page 22), Homemade French Fries (page 83), Apple Pie (page 49), and No-Churn Vanilla Ice Cream (page 6)

ALLEN LEE DAVIS ✂ July 20, 1944–July 8, 1999

Allen Lee "Tiny" Davis, who weighed around 350 pounds, was convicted of killing a pregnant woman and her two daughters and was executed in the electric chair in Florida in 1999. His execution drew criticism because the blood thinning medication he was taking caused a nose bleed while he was in the electric chair. This led to arguments against the use of electrocutions as a means of capital punishment, with people advocating for universal use of lethal injection.

Davis was the last inmate executed in Florida by an electric chair before the implementation of lethal injection. However, an inmate can still request electrocution if they so choose.

LAST MEAL: "Tiny" Davis' last meal request was the opposite of tiny: one lobster tail, fried potatoes, a half-pound of fried shrimp, six ounces of fried clams, half a loaf of garlic bread, and 32 ounces of A&W root beer.

BAKED HERB-BUTTER GARLIC BREAD

Garlic bread is often paired with Italian food, but frozen garlic bread was actually invented in Michigan in the 1970's. This recipe pumps up the savory goodness with a little bit of cheese. Feel free to add as much as you'd like!

MAKES: 10 to 12 servings | **PREP TIME:** 5 minutes | **COOK TIME:** 12 minutes

INGREDIENTS

1 loaf Italian bread

½ cup (1 stick) salted butter, at room temperature

½ tablespoon Italian seasoning

1½ teaspoons garlic powder

1 tablespoon grated Parmesan cheese

1. Preheat the oven to 375°F.

2. Split the bread lengthwise. In a small bowl, stir together the butter, Italian seasoning, garlic powder, and cheese.

3. Evenly spread the butter mixture across the cut sides of the bread. Stack the loaf halves back together and wrap in foil.

4. Bake for 12 minutes. Remove from the oven, remove foil, slice, and serve hot.

SERVE WITH: Deep-Fried Shrimp (page 44) and Homemade French Fries (page 83)

JOHN DAVID DUTY ⟶ April 25, 1952–December 16, 2010

John David Duty was an American murderer originally from Oklahoma. Duty was not initially in prison for murder, but while incarcerated at Oklahoma State Penitentiary, he held eight people hostage in the medical unit and finally released them five hours later. Duty was serving a 20-year sentence for kidnapping and rape in 1979 when the hostage situation occurred. In 2001, Duty murdered his cellmate, which resulted in an execution sentence.

He was executed by lethal injection in 2010. Duty's execution was not without controversy because of a nationwide shortage of sodium thiopental, the traditional drug used for lethal injection. The state considered using a drug that was more often used for animal euthanasia, but there was concern over its effectiveness and so Duty and two other prisoners appealed their death sentences. These appeals were unsuccessful, and Duty's execution was carried out with the replacement drug.

LAST MEAL: a double cheeseburger with mayonnaise; a foot-long hot dog with cheese, mustard, and extra onions; a cherry limeade; and a large banana shake.

CHERRY LIMEADE

This is a recipe for a classic cherry limeade—tart, sweet, and refreshing. John David Duty also requested a banana shake for his last meal. It seems he had an affinity for uniquely flavored, fruity drinks.

MAKES: 2 servings | **PREP TIME:** 10 minutes | **COOK TIME:** 10 minutes | **REFRIGERATION TIME:** 45 minutes

FOR THE LIMEADE:
- 1 cup water
- 2/3 cup sugar
- 1 cup fresh lime juice (from 9 to 12 limes)

FOR THE DRINKS:
- 1 cup water
- 3 tablespoons maraschino cherry juice
- cherries and lime wedges, for garnish
- ice

1. To make the limeade, in a medium saucepan over medium-high heat, bring the water and sugar to a simmer. Reduce the heat to medium-low and whisk to dissolve sugar. Remove from the heat and cool for about 5 minutes. Whisk in the lime juice. Cool and store in a quart-size mason jar. The mixture will keep for 7 to 10 days in the fridge.

2. To make the drinks, once the limeade is cool, add the maraschino cherry juice and water. Garnish with a lime and a cherry and serve over ice.

SERVE WITH: Hamburgers (page 113), but make them doubles and add some of your favorite cheese.

MONA FANDEY (NUR MAZNAH BINTI ISMAIL)

January 15, 1956–November 2, 2001

Nur Maznah Binti Ismail, better known as Mona Fandey, was a murderer from Malaysia, as well as a former pop singer. When she left the music business, Fandey became involved with shaman and worked with her husband and an assistant to provide her upper-class clients with black magic services. In 1993 the trio was commissioned by a politician named Mazlan Idris to help boost his success. Fandey murdered him and dismembered his body in her home with the help of her husband and assistant. After the murder, Fandey went shopping and had plastic surgery with money taken from Mazlan Idris's bank account. She was arrested and convicted in 1993 by the Temerloh High Court. The seriousness of her circumstances did not seem to phase her. In fact, during the trial, Fandey was often seen smiling and posing for photographers in her very vibrant outfits. Fandey appealed her sentence but was unsuccessful, and she was executed by hanging in 2001.

LAST MEAL: Fandey requested no last meal, but was brought a standard KFC dinner.

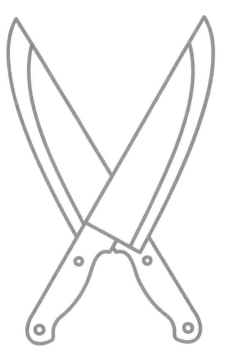

COLESLAW

Coleslaw is a Dutch term *koolsla* meaning "cabbage salad." This coleslaw recipe is a standard side in most KFC meals. See page 42 to make fried chicken.

MAKES: 6 to 8 servings | **PREP TIME:** 10 minutes

INGREDIENTS

½ cup mayonnaise

2 tablespoon sugar

1 tablespoon white vinegar

1 tablespoon apple cider vinegar

½ teaspoon pepper

¼ teaspoon salt

1 (14-ounce) package coleslaw mix

———

Stir together the mayonnaise, sugar, white vinegar, apple cider vinegar, pepper, and salt in a large bowl. Add the coleslaw mix and toss to coat. Refrigerate for at least 15 minutes before serving.

SERVE WITH: Crispy Fried Chicken (page 42) and Creamy Mashed Potatoes (page 99)

RAYMOND FERNANDEZ
December 17, 1914–March 8, 1951
MARTHA BECK
May 8, 1920–March 8, 1951

Raymond Fernandez was born in Hawaii to Spanish parents. After working for British Intelligence during World War II, he incurred a head injury in an accident on a ship bound for the United States. It has been speculated that this damage to his frontal lobe affected his sexual and social behaviors, and could be a cause of his crimes. He was arrested for theft and served some time in jail before meeting his accomplice, Martha Beck.

Beck was born six years after Fernandez in Florida, and came from a household of abuse. Beck met Fernandez after he answered her lonely hearts ad, and she abandoned her children to be with him. Fernandez saw this as the ultimate devotion, and their dysfunctional relationship eventually culminated in the murders of the two adult women and a young child. Beck was very jealous of women who came in contact with Fernandez, and it was a motive for one of the attacks.

After the murders, which occurred in two different states, neighbors became suspicious of the two women and the little girl's disappearances, and Fernandez and Beck were arrested. Sometimes called the "Lonely Hearts," the two were convicted and executed by the electric chair in 1951.

LAST MEAL: Fernandez requested an onion omelet, French fries, chocolate candy, and a Cuban cigar. Beck requested fried chicken, fried potatoes, and salad.

CARAMELIZED ONION AND CHEESE OMELET

This omelet is filled with sweet caramelized onions and Gruyère cheese. There are different preparations for an omelet. In the US, it is common for all the ingredients to be mixed together in the omelet. French omelets are soft, buttery, and are neatly folded or rolled up as they cook.

MAKES: 1 serving | **PREP TIME:** 5 minutes | **COOK TIME:** 25 minutes

INGREDIENTS

1 medium yellow onion, thinly sliced

2 teaspoons salted butter, divided

1 teaspoon olive oil

3 large eggs

¼ cup whole milk

¼ teaspoon salt

⅛ teaspoon pepper

⅓ cup shredded Gruyère cheese

1. To a medium skillet add the onion, 1 teaspoon of the butter, and oil. Cook over medium-low heat to allow the onion to cook slowly, until the onions are brown and soft, about 15 minutes. Stir occasionally to prevent burning. Remove from the heat.

2. In a small bowl, whisk together the eggs, milk, salt, and pepper. In a medium skillet, melt the remaining 1 teaspoon butter over medium-low heat. Once melted, add the egg mixture. Gently push in the sides of the eggs to help the uncooked egg to reach the heat.

3. Once the tops of the eggs have set and are not liquid, add the cheese on one side and two-thirds of the caramelized onions on the other. Carefully fold the omelet in half. Allow to finish cooking, about 3 minutes. Top with the remaining onions.

SERVE WITH: Crispy Fried Chicken (page 42), Homemade French Fries (page 83), and Crudités Platter with Herb-Dill Dip (page 57)

JOHN WAYNE GACY — March 17, 1942–May 10, 1994

John Wayne Gacy was an American serial killer from Illinois. He was known for dressing up as a clown for special events, using the name "Patches" or "Pogo," and came to be called "The Killer Clown." Gacy grew up in an abusive household, but had a close relationship with his mother and sisters despite the violence from his alcoholic father. As an adult, he managed KFC restaurants and maintained a family man appearance, but he was living a double life. Behind his upstanding citizen persona, Gacy had begun sexually assaulting boys, oftentimes paying them and giving them alcohol. Eventually he was charged and convicted of assault on a teenage boy, and served prison time. He argued his innocence throughout the whole process, and even paid a teenager to beat the victim to try to prevent him from testifying. Gacy served 18 months of his 10-year sentence. While he was incarcerated, his wife divorced him and his father died.

What is infuriating is that Gacy violated his parole and was caught, but the Iowa Board of Parole never learned of the sexual assault charges. When Gacy's parole ended, records of his previous convictions in Iowa were sealed. Thanks to this oversight, Gacy (with his mother's help) was able to purchase a home on Summerdale Avenue in Norwood Park Township, Illinois, an unincorporated part of Cook County, where he lived until his final arrest. Gacy remarried and started his own construction business. He also became active in the community and in fundraising efforts for various organizations, donning his clown costume at many events. But Gacy's actions behind the scenes were escalating. Not only was he assaulting boys and young men, he had also begun to kill. Gacy called the period of time between 1976 and 1978 his "cruising years," when most of his murders were committed. During this time he "buried" his victims in a crawl space under his house that was mainly beneath the dining room and Gacy's bedroom. Toward the end, he began putting his victims in the Des Plaines River.

Gacy's final victim was a 15-year-old pharmacy employee named Robert Jerome Piest, whose murder would eventually lead detectives to search Gacy's home and find items from his victims. Bodies were later discovered in the crawl space, on other parts of the property, and in the Des Plaines River.

Gacy was convicted of 33 murders (only 22 were identified) and sentenced to death in 1980. While imprisoned, he began to paint; many were pictures of clowns, and he sold them from prison. Gacy remained a terrible person until the end, never showing remorse for his crimes, and saying "Kiss my ass" as his final statement. He was executed in 1994 by lethal injection.

LAST MEAL: a dozen deep-fried shrimp, a bucket of KFC's original recipe chicken, French fries, a pound of strawberries, and a bottle of diet Coke.

CRISPY FRIED CHICKEN

John Wayne Gacy managed a total of three KFC restaurants in Waterloo, and no doubt became very familiar with their secret recipe. If only a fried chicken recipe had been the only secret he'd been keeping.

MAKES: 4 servings | **PREP TIME:** 25 minutes | **COOK TIME:** 18 minutes

INGREDIENTS

1 fryer chicken (3½ to 4 pounds), cut up

1¾ cups all-purpose flour, divided

3 tablespoons cornstarch

1 teaspoon garlic powder

1 teaspoon garlic salt

1 teaspoon paprika, divided

1½ teaspoons pepper, divided, plus more for seasoning

1 teaspoon poultry seasoning

1 large egg

1 egg white

½ cup water

¼ cup vodka

1 teaspoon salt, plus more for seasoning

3 cups vegetable oil, for frying

1. Remove the chicken from the fridge. Season with salt and pepper on all sides. Allow to sit at room temperature for about 20 minutes. The chicken will not be as cold, and will not lower the oil temperature as greatly.

2. In a large shallow dish, mix 1½ cups of the flour, garlic powder, garlic salt, ½ teaspoon of the paprika, 1 teaspoon of the pepper, and the poultry seasoning. In second large shallow dish, beat the egg, egg white, water, and vodka. Add the salt and remaining ¼ cup flour, ½ teaspoon pepper, and ½ teaspoon paprika.

3. Set up an assembly line starting with the wet mixture, the dry mixture, and a clean plate at the end.

4. Pour the oil into a large cast-iron skillet so it comes about 1 inch up the side. Heat over medium-high until an instant-read thermometer registers 350°F.

5. With your left hand, dip a piece of chicken into the egg mixture. Transfer to your right hand and dip it in the flour. Press the flour into the chicken so it is evenly coated. Place the chicken on the clean plate. Repeat with the remaining chicken pieces. Keeping one hand dry will be helpful to reduce sticking, and make the breading process more efficient.

6. Fry the chicken a few pieces at a time until golden brown and a thermometer inserted into chicken reads 165°F, about 7 to 8 minutes on each side. Drain on paper towel–lined plates.

DEEP-FRIED SHRIMP

Continuing on with John Wayne Gacy's gut-busting last meal, we have crispy, crunchy deep-fried shrimp. Fried shrimp is popular not only in the United States, but also in Asia—especially Japan, Korea, and Southeast Asia.

MAKES: 12 shrimp | **PREP TIME:** 10 minutes | **COOK TIME:** 5 minutes

INGREDIENTS

½ cup all-purpose flour

¼ teaspoon salt

¼ teaspoon garlic powder

¼ teaspoon onion powder

¼ teaspoon paprika

1 large egg

1 tablespoon milk

1 cup panko breadcrumbs

12 large raw shrimp, peeled, tail-on

½ cup vegetable oil

1. Place the flour, salt, garlic powder, onion powder, and paprika in a medium bowl. Stir with a fork to evenly mix.

2. Crack the egg into a medium bowl, add the milk, and beat with a fork. Next, place the panko on a plate.

3. Set up an assembly line starting with flour mixture, then the egg, and then the panko. Place a clean plate at the end.

4. Add the oil to the cast-iron skillet so it is about 1 inch up sides. If you are using a smaller or larger skillet adjust amount accordingly. Heat the oil over medium high heat until oil reaches about 350°F.

5. With your left hand, dredge a shrimp in the flour. Transfer to your right hand and dip it in the egg and then the panko.

Press the panko into the shrimp so it is evenly coated. Place the shrimp on the clean plate. Repeat with the remaining shrimp. Keeping one hand dry will help reduce sticking and make the breading process more efficient.

6. Place the shrimp in the pan using tongs. Try to keep them from touching so the pan is not too crowded and the shrimp can cook evenly. It helps to place the shrimp in a circle so you know which was in the longest and work in a circular pattern when you need to flip. Cook the shrimp 90 seconds per side. Gently flip, starting with the first shrimp you placed in the pan. If the breading begins to stick, give them a little more time.

7. Remove shrimp from the pan and place on a paper towel-lined plate.

SERVE WITH: Homemade French Fries (page 83)

THE SERIAL KILLER COOKBOOK

GUSTAVO JULIAN GARCIA

September 27, 1972–February 16, 2016

Gustavo Julian Garcia was an American murderer from Texas. He killed two people during two separate robberies and was arrested for his crimes in 1991. Prior to his execution, Garcia was given a new sentencing hearing after racist remarks surfaced that were made by the psychologist who testified. The second hearing was not in Garcia's favor and he was sentenced to death again and executed by lethal injection in 2016.

LAST MEAL: As Texas abolished last meals in 2011, Garcia received the same as the rest of the prisoners: chicken patties, macaroni and cheese, sweet peas, carrots, pinto beans, sliced bread, and a choice of water, tea, or punch to drink.

CREAMY ONE-POT MAC AND CHEESE

This is a recipe for stove-top, four-cheese macaroni and cheese. While generally thought to be an all-American dish, the origins of mac and cheese are unclear. But some say that Thomas Jefferson brought the comfort food classic to the United States after eating it in Italy. Who could blame him?

MAKES: 6 servings | **PREP TIME:** 10 minutes | **COOK TIME:** 20 minutes

INGREDIENTS

4¼ cups whole milk

2¼ cups water

1 pound large elbow pasta

4 ounces American cheese

1 cup shredded sharp cheddar cheese

½ cup shredded Monterey jack cheese

½ cup shredded Colby jack cheese

salt and pepper

1. In a large pot, stir together the milk, water, and pasta. Over medium heat, bring the mixture to a low simmer and cook for 15 to 18 minutes, stirring frequently, until the pasta is tender and the milk has reduced.

2. Turn the heat to low and gently stir in the cheeses until melted and creamy. Season with salt and pepper and serve immediately.

RONNIE LEE GARDNER ✂ January 16, 1961–June 18, 2010

Ronnie Lee Gardner was an American murderer from Utah. He came from an abusive home and as a child was exposed to drugs and crime. He spent his childhood cycling through different caregivers and was sexually abused by a number of them. He was also involved in burglaries and robberies from a young age. Gardner also was in and out of institutions, and by 20 years old he was imprisoned for robbery. While in prison, he was anything but an upstanding inmate. In fact, he successfully escaped the maximum security unit and, after recapture, led a disturbance during which inmates barricaded a cell block and set it on fire. Several years later Gardner successfully escaped from a hospital in Utah, where he'd been brought after faking an illness. Soon after his escape, Gardner robbed a Salt Lake City bar and murdered the bartender.

While Gardner was on trial for this robbery and murder, he tried to escape yet again, and shot and killed Michael Burdell an attorney in the courthouse. Gardner was eventually convicted of both murders and sentenced to death, though during his trial, some debated whether Gardner had been destined for a life of crime and violence due to his traumatic upbringing.

Gardner requested to be executed by firing squad because of his Mormon background. This type of "blood atonement" is a Mormon belief that some crimes are so severe that the blood of the perpetrator must be spilled. During the time leading up to his execution, Gardner attempted to kill another inmate and broke the glass in the prison's visitation area. His violent actions inspired the introduction of the "Ronnie Lee Gardner bill" that would allow guards to shoot unarmed prisoners attempting to escape. Further, new safety precautions were added to the courthouse after Gardener's near escape.

In 2010, Gardner's execution took place indoors in a chamber with a metal chair with restraints and rifle ports in the wall. A target was placed over his heart, and the rifles were not all loaded with real bullets so there was no way to know which officer actually delivered the fatal shot.

LAST MEAL: lobster tail, steak, apple pie with vanilla ice cream, and 7up. He also requested to watch the *Lord of the Rings* films.

APPLE PIE

This is a classic American apple pie: flaky dough baked with tender apples spiced with cinnamon and sugar. Some people might feel intimidated by pie making, but there's no need to be nervous! Start out with store-bought pie crusts and soon you'll be baking like a pro.

MAKES: 8 servings | **PREP TIME:** 15 minutes | **COOK TIME:** 30 minutes | **REST TIME:** 20 minutes

INGREDIENTS

7 cups peeled, thinly sliced, chopped Macintosh apples (about 6 to 8 apples)

1 tablespoon lemon juice

2 teaspoons ground cinnamon

1½ tablespoons all-purpose flour

¾ cup granulated sugar

¼ cup brown sugar

2 (9-inch) prepared pie crusts

½ tablespoon unsalted butter

1 egg

1 tablespoon water

1. Preheat the oven to 325°F.

2. In a large bowl, combine the apples, lemon juice, cinnamon, flour, granulated sugar, and brown sugar. Stir gently.

3. Fit one pie crust into a 9-inch pie plate. Trim the edges if needed.

4. Pour the filling into the crust and spread the apples evenly. Place the butter in the center. Place the top crust over the apples. Trim and seal the edges, and cut four slits in the top. In a small bowl, beat the egg with the water, and brush over the pie.

5. Bake at 325°F for 20 minutes. Increase the oven temperature to 400°F and bake an additional 10 minutes. Allow the pie to rest at least 20 minutes before slicing.

SERVE WITH: No-Churn Vanilla Ice Cream (page 6)

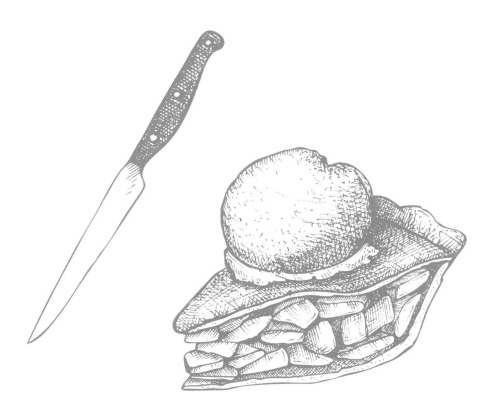

THOMAS J. GRASSO 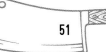 November 23, 1962-March 20, 1995

Thomas J. Grasso was an American murderer charged with killing two elderly victims. He strangled 87-year-old Hilda Johnson in her home on Christmas Eve and robbed her of what amounted to around $137. Six months later, Grasso strangled 81-year-old Leslie Holtz and stole his Social Security check. Grasso was convicted of the latter murder, but was extradited to Oklahoma to be tried for the murder of his first victim. He was executed there in 1995 by lethal injection.

LAST MEAL: two dozen steamed mussels, two dozen steamed clams with lemon, a Burger King double cheeseburger, half-dozen barbecued spareribs, two strawberry milkshakes, one-half of a pumpkin pie with whipped cream, diced strawberries, and a can of SpaghettiOs with meatballs. He was upset because he received a can of regular spaghetti with meatballs. Grasso used his last statement to air his grievances: "I did not get my SpaghettiOs, I got spaghetti. I want the press to know this."

HOMEMADE SPAGHETTI-OH'S

Grasso was less than thrilled with his regular canned spaghetti, but this recipe for homemade Spaghetti-Oh's is a giant step up from the canned childhood favorite, and it's almost just as easy to make.

MAKES: 2 servings | **PREP TIME:** 5 minutes | **COOK TIME:** 10 minutes

INGREDIENTS

1 (15-ounce) can tomato sauce

2½ tablespoons milk

½ teaspoon onion powder

½ teaspoon salt

1½ teaspoons salted butter

1½ tablespoons sugar

½ cup large pasta rings

½ cup small pasta rings

1. Add the tomato sauce, milk, onion powder, salt, butter, and sugar to a medium saucepan over medium heat. Allow the sauce to come to a low simmer and the butter to melt. Lightly simmer for about 5 minutes.

2. In a small pot, cook the pasta until tender. The pasta is small and this will only take a few minutes, so check frequently to prevent it from overcooking.

3. Drain the pasta and add to the sauce. Stir gently to coat.

SERVE WITH: Strawberry Milkshakes (page 82)

FRITZ HAARMANN

 October 25, 1879–April 15, 1925

Fritz Haarmann was a German serial killer also known as the "Vampire of Hanover," the "Butcher of Hanover," and the "Wolf Man." These nicknames came from his particularly gruesome signature of biting his victims' throats (which he called "love bites"...yuck). He also dismembered and mutilated his victims and was found guilty of 24 murders of young boys and men, but there are likely more.

Haarmann was first arrested in 1896 and, after further offenses, was placed in a psychiatric hospital for being "incurably deranged." After less than a year in the institution, Haarmann escaped with the help of his mother. He later became engaged to a young woman and served in the military, but was discharged due to health conditions. Upon his return home, his fiancée must have sensed what a creep Haarmann was because she broke off their engagement. From then on, Haarmann began committing crimes like burglary, theft, and embezzlement. Haarmann served time in jail for several of these crimes and even became a police informant, a position that he used to direct attention away from the assaults and murders he'd begun to commit.

I'll spare you the details of Haarmann's murder spree, because he was truly disgusting, and this is, after all, a cookbook. Police became suspicious of Haarmann when they observed him loitering around Hanover's train station trying to find a new victim. He was eventually arrested when a young man informed the police that Haarmann had been assaulting him for four days. The police searched Haarmann's apartment and discovered a bloodstained space that contained many items from previous victims, evidence that sealed Haarmann's fate.

Despite his multiple stays at psychiatric facilities, Haarmann was declared competent to stand trial, convicted of 24 murders, and sentenced to die. Haarmann was beheaded by guillotine in Hanover prison.

LAST MEAL: a cigar and a cup of Brazilian coffee.

DOUBLE-CHOCOLATE COFFEE PUDDING

I've turned Haarmann's cup of coffee into a chocolate coffee pudding, a dessert that everyone can enjoy. And if you're so inclined, it would taste lovely with coffee and a cigar.

MAKES: 6 servings | **PREP TIME:** 15 minutes

INGREDIENTS

1 (5.9-ounce) box instant chocolate pudding

1½ cups cold whole milk

¼ cup cold coffee

1 teaspoon finely ground coffee

1 tablespoon prepared chocolate fudge topping

In a medium bowl, whisk the instant pudding with milk and coffee. Once pudding thickens, stir in coffee and fudge. Refrigerate for 15 minutes before serving.

BRUNO RICHARD HAUPTMANN

November 26, 1899–April 3, 1936

Bruno Richard Hauptmann was born in Germany and eventually made his way to the United States after WWI by illegally stowing away on an ocean liner. Years later, he committed "the crime of the century": the kidnapping and murder of the Lindbergh baby. Charles Lindbergh was a famous American aviator, and the disappearance of his young son created a media firestorm. After a $50,000 ransom was delivered, the poor baby's body was found in the woods just 4 miles from the Lindberghs' home. Hauptmann was arrested for the kidnapping after spending one of the ransom bills at a gas station.

His attorney claimed the case evidence was circumstantial, but the appeal failed. Hauptmann, who maintained his innocence until the very end, was executed in the electric chair in 1936 in New Jersey. His memorial service was a private affair for his widow, but outside there was a crowd of around 2,000 people.

LAST MEAL: His (somewhat balanced) request was celery, olives, buttered peas, chicken, French fries, cherries, and a slice of cake for dessert.

CRUDITÉS PLATTER WITH HERB-DILL DIP

"Crudité platter" is just an impressive way to say: fresh-cut veggies arranged on a platter and served with some type of vegetable dip. I've given a list of my favorite veggies to use on a crudité platter, but feel free to swap with your own favorites!

MAKES: about 1 cup dip | **PREP TIME:** 35 minutes

FOR THE DIP:

8 ounces cream cheese, softened

½ cup mayonnaise

¼ cup sour cream

1 tablespoon finely chopped fresh dill

1 tablespoon finely chopped fresh parsley

½ teaspoon onion powder

½ teaspoon garlic powder

¼ teaspoon salt

¼ teaspoon pepper

FOR THE CRUDITÉS:

carrots

cucumber

bell pepper

green onion

cherry tomatoes

———

To make the dip, in a medium bowl, stir together all the ingredients until smooth. Cover and Refrigerate for about 30 minutes before serving. Serve with chopped veggies.

SERVE WITH: Homemade French Fries (page 83), Crispy Fried Chicken (page 42), Single-Olive Tapenade (page 19), and Chocolate Layer Cake (page 102)

PETER KÜRTEN — May 26, 1883–July 2, 1931

Peter Kürten was a German serial killer called the "Vampire of Düsseldorf" and the "Düsseldorf Monster." Kürten grew up in an abusive home, and resorted to petty crime at a young age. He abused and killed animals from a young age as well, and was an arsonist. Upon arrest, Kürten was charged with nine murders and seven attempted murders, though he freely admitted to 68 total crimes. The majority took place from 1913 to 1929, with victims ranging in age from 5 to 80 years old.

As with Fritz Haarmann (page 54), I'll spare you the details of this guy's terrifying crimes. After one of his victims escaped and was able to lead police to Kürten's home, Kürten admitted to his wife (yes, this creep was married the whole time he was assaulting and killing people) that he was the Vampire of Düsseldorf. He encouraged her to turn him in so that she could collect the reward money for his capture. The next day his wife did just that, and Kürten was arrested, charged, convicted, and sentenced to death.

During Kürten's incarceration, leading up to his trial, he was interviewed extensively by Dr. Karl Berg, who determined that Kürten was competent to stand trial even though he was an extreme sexual sadist. At the trial, he had to sit in a guarded cage to protect him from any attacks by the enraged families of his victims. Kürten was executed by guillotine in 1931, a method which excited him. After his death his head was mummified and studied, though his brain revealed no explanations for his horrific actions. If you'd like to be sufficiently spooked, you can see it for yourself at Ripley's Believe It or Not! in Wisconsin Dells, Wisconsin.

LAST MEAL: two portions of Wiener schnitzel, fried potatoes, and a bottle of white wine.

FRIED POTATOES AND ONIONS

These fried potatoes are prepared the German way. The German name is *Bratkartoffeln*, but these potatoes are very similar to what we call home fries is the United States.

MAKES: 1 serving | **PREP TIME:** 5 minutes | **COOK TIME:** 10 minutes

INGREDIENTS

2 medium russet potatoes

2 tablespoons salted butter

¼ cup chopped white onion

salt and pepper

paprika

1. Peel the potatoes if desired. Cut in half lengthwise and slice ¼-inch half-moons. Pat the potatoes dry after slicing.

2. In a medium cast-iron skillet, add the butter, onions, and potatoes. Spread the potatoes in an even layer and allow them to cook over medium to medium-low heat for about 5 minutes before flipping. You want the heat low enough so that the potatoes and onions do not burn but get nice and brown.

3. Flip the potatoes to allow the other side to brown. Cook for about 5 minutes. Add more butter if needed.

4. Season to taste with salt, pepper, and paprika.

HOMEMADE GERMAN SCHNITZEL

Homemade schnitzel can come together pretty quickly due to the thin cut of meat. You can coat the meat in as much batter as you like. Some people prefer a thicker coat while others like a thinner coat.

MAKES: 4 servings | **PREP TIME:** 15 minutes | **COOK TIME:** 10 minutes

INGREDIENTS

- 4 boneless thin pork steaks
- 1 teaspoon salt
- 1 teaspoon black pepper
- ½ cup all-purpose flour
- ½ teaspoon salt
- 1 large egg, lightly beaten

- ¼ cup whole milk
- ¾ cup unseasoned breadcrumbs
- 2 tablespoons salted butter
- 2 tablespoons olive oil
- lemon wedges, for serving

1. Remove pork from the fridge. Salt and pepper on both sides of the pork. Allow to sit for about 10 minutes. Bringing the pork to room temperature means it will not lower the oil temperature as greatly.

2. In a large shallow dish, mix flour and salt. In another dish, beat the egg and milk.

3. Set up the stations in a line starting with wet mixture, the dry mixture, and a clean plate at the end of the assembly line.

4. With your left hand dip pork into the egg mixture. Transfer to your right hand and dip it in the flour. Press the flour into the steak so it is evenly coated. Place pork on the clean plate. Repeat with remaining pork pieces. Keeping one hand dry will be helpful to reduce sticking, and make the breading process more efficient.

5. Add butter and oil into a large cast-iron skillet and heat on medium high heat. Add pork to the skillet and cook over medium high heat. Cook pork 2-3 minutes per side. Remove from skillet and serve with lemon wedges.

TIMOTHY McVEIGH   April 23, 1968–June 11, 2001

Timothy McVeigh was an American domestic terrorist and mass murderer responsible for the 1995 Oklahoma City bombing, which killed 168 people and injured more than 680 others. The bombing was the deadliest attack on American soil until September 11, and is still the deadliest act of domestic terrorism.

When he was young, McVeigh was interested in computer programing and guns, and was a strong believer in gun rights. In 1988, he joined the army and was part of Operation Desert Storm; he was honorably discharged in 1991. After leaving the military, McVeigh struggled with debt and blamed the majority of it on the government and taxes. The government, he believed, was the ultimate bully. When the United States government laid siege to a religious compound in Waco, Texas, McVeigh drove there to show his support for the cult members and was very critical of how the FBI handled the entire situation. He also became very active in the gun show circuit, which allowed him to travel to many different states. McVeigh moved to Arizona for a short period of time, and then finally to Michigan, where he learned how to make explosive devices and plotted to bomb a federal building.

On April 19, 1995, McVeigh bombed the federal building in Oklahoma. This building had a daycare center in it, and 19 children were among the many victims. McVeigh was arrested within days of the bombing after the identification number of the vehicle parked outside the building was traced back to an alias he used, and he was eventually identified. McVeigh was indicted for his crimes in 1995, and in 1997 he was found guilty and sentenced to death. The trial was in Colorado, but he was moved to Indiana for the execution. McVeigh was executed by lethal injection in 2001. He showed very little remorse for his crimes, and expressed his regret that he was not able to destroy the entire building. He had hoped to start a revolution against the government.

LAST MEAL: two pints of mint chocolate chip ice cream.

MINT CHIP ICE CREAM

My recipe uses natural mint flavoring and no artificial colors. Fun fact: Mint chocolate chip was invented in the 1970s by a culinary student hoping to win a contest to have her ice cream featured at Princess Anne and Captain Mark Phillips' wedding!

MAKES: 4 servings | **PREP TIME:** 15 minutes | **FREEZER TIME:** 12 hours

INGREDIENTS

2 cups heavy cream

1 (14-ounce) can sweetened condensed milk

1¼ teaspoons peppermint extract

½ teaspoon vanilla extract

1 cup chopped semi-sweet chocolate or semi-sweet chocolate chips

1. In a stand mixer with the whisk attachment, whip the cream at high speed until stiff peaks form, 2 to 3 minutes.

2. In a medium bowl, stir together the condensed milk, peppermint, and vanilla. Gently fold the whipped cream into the condensed milk mixture. Stir in the chocolate.

3. Pour the cream mixture into a 9 x 5-inch loaf pan. Make sure the cream is sitting evenly in the pan. Cover tightly. Freeze at least 12 hours before serving. Best served no more than 30 to 45 days after the first freezing.

ERIC NANCE ✂ January 9, 1960–November 28, 2005

Eric Nance was an American murderer who raped and killed an 18-year-old girl named Julie Heath. In 1994, Nance was convicted of the murder and sentenced to die by lethal injection. There was a short stay placed on his execution due to allegations of a low IQ, but it was lifted in 2005. While imprisoned, Nance wrote poetry. One of his poems was recorded and set to music by the Celtic Tenors. Nance was executed in Arkansas in 2005.

LAST MEAL: two bacon cheeseburgers, French fries, two pints of chocolate chip cookie dough ice cream, and two Cokes.

CHOCOLATE CHIP COOKIE DOUGH CHOCOLATE CHIP ICE CREAM

I've made this beloved flavor as easy as possible to make thanks to store-bought cookie dough topping!

MAKES: 6 servings | **PREP TIME:** 15 minutes | **FREEZER TIME:** 12 hours

INGREDIENTS

2 cups heavy cream

1 (14-ounce) can sweetened condensed milk

½ teaspoon vanilla extract

½ cup chopped semi-sweet chocolate or semi-sweet chocolate chips

1¼ cups prepared cookie dough topping

1. In a stand mixer with the whisk attachment, whip the cream at high speed until stiff peaks form, 2 to 3 minutes.

2. In a medium bowl, stir together the condensed milk and vanilla. Gently fold the whipped cream into condensed milk mixture. Stir in the chocolate and the cookie dough.

3. Pour the cream mixture into a 9 x 5-inch loaf pan. Make sure the cream is sitting evenly in the pan. Cover tightly. Freeze at least 12 hours before serving. Best served no more than 30 to 45 days after the first freezing.

SERVE WITH: Homemade French Fries (page 83)

CHARLES PEACE ✦ May 14, 1832–February 25, 1879

Charles Peace was a serial killer from the United Kingdom. He began to commit burglaries and petty crimes after being crippled in an accident at the age of 14. When Peace was 44 years old he committed his first murder after a policeman tried to arrest Peace during a bout of late-night trespassing. Peace escaped and another man took the blame for the crime. Soon after he became obsessed with his neighbor's wife, despite her and her husband's numerous attempts to thwart Peace's advances. The family even put cards in his garden asking him to stay away. Unfortunately, their pleas didn't work, and Peace shot the husband and went on the run after the murder. He was eventually caught, and during the trial there was an attempt to insinuate that a close friendship existed between Peace and his neighbor's wife, but nothing was ever proven. Peace was found guilty and died by hanging.

LAST MEAL: eggs and lots of salty bacon.

OVEN-BAKED BACON

This recipe is for perfectly cooked bacon in the oven, which reduces painful grease splatters and frees up the stove so you can simultaneously cook your favorite omelet or eggs.

MAKES: 4 servings | **PREP TIME:** 5 minutes | **COOK TIME:** 20 minutes

INGREDIENTS

1 pound thick-sliced bacon

---

1. Preheat the oven to 400°F.

2. Line a rimmed baking sheet with foil and place a metal oven-safe cooling rack on top.

3. Place the bacon strips on the rack and make sure they are not overlapping. If you do not have a cooling rack, just skip it, but you will need to flip the bacon halfway through cooking.

4. Bake 18 to 22 minutes depending on how crisp you like your bacon. Start checking around 16 minutes to make sure it is not burning.

5. When the bacon has finished cooking, remove it from the rack, and place on a paper towel-lined plate.

SERVE WITH: Caramelized Onion and Cheese Omelet (page 39)

RICKY RAY RECTOR

January 12, 1950–January 24, 1992

Ricky Ray Rector was an American murderer from Arkansas. Rector shot three people, killing one, outside of a dance hall in 1981. He hid for a few days, but finally agreed to speak with Officer Robert Martin because Rector had known the policeman since he was a child. Rector shot the officer, left the house, and then shot himself in the head near his mother's backyard. Officer Martin was killed, but Rector survived with extensive frontal lobe damage.

Despite his brain damage, Rector stood trial. His defense objected, but the state determined that he was not impaired enough to avoid going to trail. Still, the disagreement over Rector's mental capacity continued even after his conviction and death sentence. It was, at the time, not thought that his type of brain damage fit the same laws as a person with a cognitive impairment. At the time of Rector's execution by lethal injection, Bill Clinton flew to Arkansas during his presidential campaign to make sure the procedure took place. This was Clinton's attempt to show he wasn't soft on crime, though it was a decision that continues to be highly criticized by people who oppose the death penalty.

LAST MEAL: steak, fried chicken, cherry Kool-Aid, and a pecan pie. Rector did not eat the pie and told officials that he was "saving it for later," a moment that was later cited as evidence of Rector's lack of mental capacity.

PECAN PIE

For this simple recipe of sweet pecans baked in a flaky pie crust, the filling calls for light corn syrup, but dark works as well for a more robust flavor.

MAKES: 8 servings | **PREP TIME:** 5 minutes | **COOK TIME:** 65 minutes

INGREDIENTS

1 cup light corn syrup, or something similar

3 large eggs

¾ cup granulated sugar

¼ cup brown sugar

3 tablespoons melted unsalted butter

1 teaspoon vanilla extract

1⅓ cups chopped pecans

1 (9-inch) frozen deep-dish pie crust

---

1. Preheat the oven to 350°F.

2. In a medium bowl, stir together the corn syrup, eggs, granulated sugar, brown sugar, melted butter, and vanilla. Gently stir in the pecans and pour the filling into the pie crust.

3. Bake 65 to 70 minutes, until the top is caramelized. Cool for at least 2 to 3 hours before serving so the pie sets.

DANNY ROLLING May 26, 1954–October 25, 2006

Danny Rolling was an American serial killer from Florida known as the "Gainesville Ripper." Rolling had an abusive father and began engaging in robberies and spying on women as a teenager. As an adult, he couldn't hold a steady job.

Rolling's murder and burglary spree began in Gainesville in August 1990. He murdered five college students within the span of four days. Rolling would position his victims' bodies in poses to create shock value, and this drove the media into a frenzy. He later claimed to be motivated by fame, wanting to become a "superstar" like Ted Bundy (gross).

Rolling was initially arrested for burglary, and during that investigation it became clear that his tools matched evidence left at the Florida crime scenes. It also came out that Rolling was responsible for a previously unsolved triple murder from 1989. He was sentenced to death in 1994 and was executed by lethal injection in 2006.

LAST MEAL: lobster tail, butterfly shrimp, baked potato, strawberry cheesecake, and sweet tea.

THE SERIAL KILLER COOKBOOK

NO-BAKE STRAWBERRY CHEESECAKE

Do not use low-fat or fat-free cream cheese for this recipe, as the cheesecake will not be as creamy.

MAKES: 8 servings | **PREP TIME:** 15 minutes | **REFRIGERATION TIME:** 8 hours

FOR THE CHEESECAKE:

24 ounces whole-fat cream cheese, at room temperature

1¼ cups confectioner's sugar

½ tablespoon vanilla extract

½ tablespoon lemon juice

⅛ teaspoon salt

1¼ cups heavy whipping cream

1 prepared or homemade graham cracker pie crust

FOR THE TOPPING:

1 pound fresh strawberries, hulled and chopped

⅛ cup granulated sugar

1½ tablespoons cornstarch

2 tablespoons cup water

---

1. To make the cheesecake, add the cream cheese and confectioner's sugar to a stand mixer with the paddle attachment. Beat at medium-high speed until smooth, about 2 minutes. Add the vanilla, lemon juice, and salt, and stir to combine.

2. Switch the mixer to the whisk attachment. Add the heavy cream and beat until mixture becomes thick and starts to become stiff.

3. Pour the filling into the pie crust and refrigerate for 8 hours.

4. To make the topping, in a medium saucepan, add the strawberries, sugar, cornstarch, and water. Bring to a low simmer over medium heat and allow the berries to break up, about 5 minutes. Once the mixture thickens to coat the back of a spoon, remove it from the heat.

5. Refrigerate until you are ready to serve the cheesecake. Spoon the berries over the top.

HOMEMADE CRUST OPTION

INGREDIENTS

1 ½ cups crushed graham crackers

7 tablespoons unsalted butter, melted

¼ cup granulated sugar

In a mixing bowl, mix together the crushed crackers, sugar, and butter. Press the mixture into and up the sides of a 9-inch pie pan. Place in the fridge to chill for 90 minutes.

CLASSIC SOUTHERN SWEET TEA

If you don't have a front porch...no worries! You don't need to sit your pitcher of sweet tea out on the wraparound in order to get that classic flavor. This recipe will hit the spot no matter where you live.

MAKES: 1 gallon | **PREP:** 5 minutes | **COOK TIME:** 10 minutes

INGREDIENTS

5 black tea bags

1 gallon of water, divided

1 cup granulated sugar

lemon wedges

---

1. Boil ½ gallon of water in a pot. Once it boils, remove from heat and add tea bags. Let the tea steep for 5 minutes.

2. Remove tea bags and return the pot to the heat. Add sugar and simmer to dissolve the sugar solids. Remove from heat and add the additional ½ gallon of water. Store in the fridge till chilled. Serve on ice with lemon wedges.

MICHAEL BRUCE ROSS

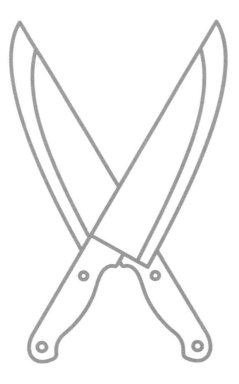 July 26, 1959–May 13, 2005

Michael Bruce Ross, possessor of three first names, was an American serial killer from Connecticut. He confessed to the rape and murder of eight young women, but was only convicted for four of them. It is thought that he is responsible for other rapes and murders in different states.

Ross came from an abusive home, and he stalked women during his college years, eventually escalating to rape and murder. He was sentenced to death in 1987, and was executed in 2005 by lethal injection. It is reported that Ross supported his own sentence and execution, but was not in favor of the death penalty in other cases. He was given the nickname "The Roadside Strangler" by a British film crew making a 1995 television piece on serial killers. However, American press and local law enforcement did not use this nickname at all during Ross's trial, imprisonment, and execution.

LAST MEAL: Ross did not request a last meal and was served the prison dinner of turkey à la king with rice, mixed vegetables, white bread, fruit, and a beverage.

CHICKEN À LA KING

I've put a more modern spin on turkey à la king by swapping the meat for chicken. This recipe is flavorful, creamy, and oh so satisfying! Enjoy!

MAKES: 4 servings | **PREP TIME:** 10 minutes | **COOK TIME:** 20 minutes

INGREDIENTS

1 pound boneless skinless chicken breasts

3 tablespoons salted butter, divided

1 cup sliced mushrooms

1 red bell pepper, chopped

⅓ cup all-purpose flour

½ teaspoon paprika

1½ cups whole milk

1⅓ cups chicken broth

salt and pepper

thick-sliced bread, such as sourdough, for serving

---

1. Season the chicken breasts with salt and pepper.

2. In a large rimmed skillet, melt 1 tablespoon of butter and cook the chicken breasts over medium-high heat until the internal temperature reaches 165°F, about 4 minutes per side. Remove from the pan and cut into bite-sized pieces.

3. In the same skillet, melt the remaining 2 tablespoons butter over medium heat and then add the mushrooms and bell peppers. Sauté until the peppers are tender and mushrooms begin to soften, about 3 minutes. Sprinkle the flour and paprika over the veggies and gently stir to coat.

4. Add the milk and chicken broth and gently stir. Add the chopped chicken back to the pan. Allow mixture to simmer and thicken for about 10 minutes over medium heat. Be careful to watch the chicken and lower the heat if needed to prevent burning. Season with salt and pepper.

5. Serve over thick-sliced toasted bread.

GARY CARL SIMMONS, JR. ✧ November 18, 1962–June 20, 2012

Gary Carl Simmons, Jr., is an American murderer from Mississippi. In 1996, he and his former brother-in-law, Timothy Milano, kidnapped a man (to whom they owed weed money) and the man's 18-year-old girlfriend. They shot the man, dismembered his body, and threw the pieces into a bayou with hopes that alligators would eat them. Simmons and his accomplice raped the girlfriend, but she eventually escaped. Her testimony would ultimately solve the case and convict Simmons and Timothy Milano (Milano received life in prison).

Simmons was sentenced to die in 1997. In 2012 he was executed by lethal injection in Mississippi. Simmons ate only around half of his insane last meal.

LAST MEAL: Simmons requested an almost 29,000-calorie meal of one Pizza Hut medium Super Supreme Deep Dish pizza with double portions of mushrooms, onions, jalapeños, and pepperoni; a second pizza with three cheeses, olives, bell pepper, tomato, garlic, and Italian sausage; 10 (8-ounce) packages of Parmesan cheese; 10 (8-ounce) packages of ranch dressing; one family-size bag of nacho-cheese Doritos; 8 ounces of jalapeño nacho cheese; 4 ounces of sliced jalapeños; two large strawberry shakes; two 20-ounce cherry Cokes; one super-size order of McDonald's fries with extra ketchup and mayonnaise; and two pints of strawberry ice cream.

NO-CHURN FRESH STRAWBERRY ICE CREAM

Since Simmons seemed to have affinity for strawberry frozen desserts (along with ranch dressing, but we'll ignore that one), this recipe is for strawberry ice cream and strawberry milkshakes.

MAKES: 4 servings | **PREP TIME:** 15 minutes | **FREEZER TIME:** 12 hours

INGREDIENTS

2 cups heavy cream

1 (14-ounce) can sweetened condensed milk

½ teaspoon vanilla extract

1 cup chopped fresh strawberries

1. In a stand mixer with the whisk attachment, whip the cream at high speed until stiff peaks form, 2 to 3 minutes.

2. In a medium bowl, stir together the condensed milk and vanilla. Gently fold the whipped cream into the condensed milk mixture. Stir in the berries.

3. Pour the cream mixture into a 9 x 5-inch loaf pan. Make sure the cream is sitting evenly in the pan. Cover tightly. Freeze at least 12 hours before serving. Best served no more than 30 to 45 days from the first freezing.

STRAWBERRY MILKSHAKES

Did you know that milkshakes initially contained alcohol? It's true — it was not until the early part of the century that the alcohol was removed and different favoring became available. However, if you spike your strawberry milkshake with a little something something — no judgment here!

MAKES: 2 servings | **PREP TIME:** 5 minutes

INGREDIENTS

4 scoops of No-Churn Fresh Strawberry Ice Cream (page 81)

¼ cup chopped strawberries

1 cup whole milk

Place all the ingredients into a blender and mix until smooth.

SERVE WITH: Homemade French Fries (page 83) are the perfect salty counterpoint to a sweet strawberry milkshake.

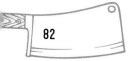

PERRY SMITH
October 27, 1928–April 14, 1965

RICHARD HICKOCK
June 6, 1931–April 14, 1965

Perry Smith and Richard Hickock were American mass murderers responsible for the Clutter family deaths in Kansas in 1959. Smith came from an abusive home, and Hickock was poor growing up and suffered from head injuries after a car crash. Smith met Hickock in prison and together they plotted to commit robbery after they both got out. The duo decided to rob the Clutter family after hearing that there was a safe in the home containing a large amount of cash. After invading the home in November 1959 and discovering that there was no safe at all, Hickock and Smith murdered Herbert, Bonnie, Nancy, and Kenyon Clutter.

Smith and Hickock were on the run for about six weeks before they were caught in Las Vegas. During interviews, both men had different accounts of what actually happened at the Clutter house. Prior to their executions, Smith and Hickock spoke to author Truman Capote, who interviewed them extensively for the true-crime book *In Cold Blood*. Smith was even said to have developed a friendship with the late author. Smith and Hickock were both executed by hanging in 1965.

LAST MEAL: shrimp, French fries, garlic bread, ice cream, and strawberries with whipped cream.

HOMEMADE FRENCH FRIES

These are deliciously salty, thin-cut French fries. You might be surprised by the short ingredient list, but a simple recipe is often the best kind. Plus, with homemade fries, you'll be able to control how crispy you make them!

MAKES: 2 to 3 servings | **PREP TIME:** 10 minutes | **COOK TIME:** 25 minutes

INGREDIENTS

4 large russet potatoes, peeled

1 quart vegetable oil

salt

1. Trim about ¼ to ½ inch off the ends of the potatoes to get the square look on the end of the fries. This is optional, and just creates a shape.

2. Slice the potatoes in half lengthwise, then cut into ¼ inch lengthwise rounds. Slice each round into strips. Place the fries in a bowl of cold water for a few minutes. This will help prevent sticking. Pat dry on a paper towel–lined plate.

3. In a heavy skillet, heat the oil to 275°F as measured on an instant-read thermometer. This will be the temperature for the first fry to cook the potato. The second fry will be at a higher heat and will make the potato crispy.

4. Cook the potatoes in batches of 15 to 20 depending on the size of your skillet. It is important that the potatoes are not crowded. Cook for about 4 minutes and remove to a paper towel–lined plate.

5. Increase the heat to bring oil to 350°F. Cook the fries in batches again for about 2 minutes or until golden. Transfer to a paper towel–lined plate. Sprinkle with salt.

SERVE WITH: Deep-Fried Shrimp (page 44), Baked Herb-Butter Garlic Bread (page 31), and No-Churn Vanilla Ice Cream (page 6)

THE SERIAL KILLER COOKBOOK

RUTH SNYDER ⟶ March 27, 1895–January 12, 1928

Ruth Snyder was an American murderer from New York. Snyder and her lover, Henry Judd Gray, a corset salesman, were charged, convicted, and sentenced to death for the murder of Snyder's husband, Albert. Albert was still enamored with his late fiancée, hanging her picture in their home and naming his boat after her. Snyder grew tired of playing second fiddle to a woman who'd been dead for 10 years and began to plot his demise. She decided to take an insurance policy out on her husband that would increase in payout in the event of a violent death.

Snyder attempted to murder her husband seven—that's right, *seven*—times, but he survived each attempt. Ultimately, Snyder and her lover were able to strangle Albert in 1927, and tried to cover their tracks by staging a burglary. Police investigating the crime were suspicious of Snyder, who wasn't acting like a traumatized widow, and soon discovered the supposedly stolen property inside the house. Both Snyder and Gray were arrested.

The former lovers turned on each other, and both were eventually convicted and sentenced to death. Snyder was executed by the electric chair, and during the execution a portion was caught on film with a small plate camera that was smuggled in by a reporter. The photo is currently in possession of the Smithsonian's Museum of Natural History.

LAST MEAL: chicken Parmesan with alfredo pasta, ice cream, two milkshakes, and a 12-pack of grape soda

CHICKEN PARMESAN WITH FETTUCCINE ALFREDO

This delicious bastardization of Italian cuisine is the ultimate rich, yummy comfort food.

MAKES: 4 to 6 servings | **PREP TIME:** 15 minutes | **COOK TIME:** 35 minutes

FOR THE CHICKEN:

4 boneless skinless chicken breasts

¾ cup all-purpose flour

½ cup grated Parmesan cheese

1 teaspoon cornstarch

¼ teaspoon onion powder

¼ teaspoon garlic powder

1 teaspoon salt

1 teaspoon pepper

2 eggs

1 tablespoon water

vegetable oil, as needed for frying

1 cup prepared marinara sauce

½ cup shredded mozzarella cheese

FOR THE PASTA:

1 pound fettuccine

5 tablespoons salted butter

2 cloves garlic, minced

1¼ cups heavy cream

1 cup grated Parmesan cheese

½ teaspoon pepper

---

1. To make the chicken, in a large shallow dish, stir together the flour, Parmesan, cornstarch, onion powder, garlic powder, salt and pepper. In a medium dish, beat the eggs and water.

2. Set up an assembly line starting with wet mixture, then the dry mixture, and a clean plate at the end.

3. Pour enough oil into a large cast-iron skillet so that it comes about 1 inch up the sides. Heat over medium high until an instant-read thermometer registers 350°F.

4. With your left hand, dip the chicken into the egg mixture. Transfer to your right hand and dip it in the flour. Press the flour into the chicken so it is evenly coated. Place the chicken on the clean plate. Repeat with the remaining chicken. Keeping one hand dry will be helpful to reduce sticking, and make the breading process more efficient.

5. Fry the chicken until golden brown and a thermometer inserted into the chicken reads 165°F, about 5 to 6 minutes on each side. Remove to a paper towel-lined plate. Allow the chicken to rest as you prepare the pasta.

6. To make the pasta, cook the fettuccine according to the package directions.

7. While the pasta cooks, prepare the sauce. In a large rimmed skillet, heat the butter over medium heat and add the garlic. Cook for about 1 minute, until fragrant, and add the cream. Let the cream cook and reduce for about 5 minutes.

8. Add the Parmesan cheese and whisk until smooth. Add the pepper and pasta and toss to coat.

9. To serve, plate the pasta and top with chicken and a little marinara sauce and mozzarella cheese.

SERVE WITH: No-Churn Vanilla Ice Cream (page 6) and Strawberry Milkshakes (page 82) for a similar meal to Snyder's. If you aren't keen on that extra dose of dairy, I suggest pairing this dish with a side of Baked Herb-Butter Garlic Bread (page 31).

GERALD STANO ~~✦~~ September 12, 1951–March 23, 1998

Gerald Stano was an American serial killer from New York. He was so severely neglected when his mother gave him up at 6 months old, that doctors stated he was basically unadoptable. After recovery, Stano was eventually adopted by a nurse and her husband. Though the Stanos were good parents, Gerald did not thrive in their care. He wet the bed, was bullied, stole money, and didn't graduate high school until the age of 21.

Stano was allegedly responsible for the murders of more than 40 women. He was charged with nine murders and sentenced to death by the electric chair. There was controversy surrounding his conviction because it was thought that he confessed to crimes he did not commit, and that police were even feeding him details of unsolved homicides. Despite the questions, Stano's execution was carried out in 1998.

LAST MEAL: Delmonico steak, a baked potato with sour cream and bacon bits, tossed salad with blue cheese dressing, lima beans, a half-gallon of mint chocolate-chip ice cream, and a two-liter bottle of Pepsi.

SALT-CRUSTED BAKED POTATO

Traditional baked potato recipes direct the potato to be wrapped in foil, which does not allow the potato skin to crisp. Tossing the foil, and rubbing the potato with oil and coarse salt give it a crisp and salty skin. Add whatever toppings you like best.

MAKES: 4 servings | **PREP TIME:** 5 minutes | **COOK TIME:** 45 minutes

INGREDIENTS

4 medium russet potatoes

2 tablespoons olive oil

1 ½ tablespoons coarse sea salt

1. Preheat the oven to 425°F. Line a baking sheet with foil and place the potatoes on the baking sheet.

2. Pierce the potatoes a few times with a fork. Rub each potato with ½ tablespoon of olive oil and then rub with sea salt.

3. Bake for 45 minutes, until the skin is crisp and the inside is fork tender. Remove and serve with butter.

SERVE WITH: Mint Chip Ice Cream (page 64)

CHARLES STARKWEATHER November 24, 1938–June 25, 1959

Charles Starkweather was an American spree killer. At 19, he traveled with his 14-year-old girlfriend across Nebraska and Wyoming, murdering 11 people. Starkweather's 1958 spree has been the inspiration of multiple films including *Natural Born Killers*.

Starkweather's girlfriend claimed that she was held hostage and that he threatened to kill her family if she didn't go with him. However, Starkweather had already shot both her mother and stepfather and stabbed her baby sister before his spree, and so authorities didn't believe her allegations. She was convicted, but later paroled.

Charles Starkweather was executed in Nebraska by the electric chair in 1959.

LAST MEAL: cold cuts.

COLD-CUT SANDWICHES

This makes a deluxe cold-cut sandwich with ham, turkey, roast beef, cheese, lettuce, tomato, mayo, vinegar, and a little seasoning.

MAKES: 4 servings | **PREP TIME:** 10 minutes

INGREDIENTS

4 (8-inch) sub rolls

mustard

mayonnaise

romaine lettuce

½ pound shaved turkey breast

½ pound shaved ham

8 slices Colby jack cheese

sliced tomatoes

---

1. Slice sub rolls in half lengthwise. You can toast them if you'd like.

2. Spread the mustard on one half of each roll and mayonnaise on the other half. Add the lettuce to one side of all the rolls.

3. Add the meat. The subs can be a mix of turkey and ham, or just one or the other. Add 2 slices of cheese to each sandwich.

4. Top with tomatoes and place the top half of each roll on the subs.

PABLO LUCIO VASQUEZ ✦ August 11, 1977–April 6, 2016

Pablo Lucio Vasquez was an American murderer from Texas. Vasquez got the nickname "The Vampire Killer" because he drank his victim's blood. He met this victim, a 12-year-old boy, at a party. Vasquez did a number of horrifying things to the child before hiding the body beneath pieces of aluminum.

Vasquez was arrested after police received an anonymous tip, and admitted that the devil had told him to decapitate the boy. Vasquez was tried and sentenced to death in 1999, and his execution by lethal injection was carried out in 2016.

LAST MEAL: Texas stopped giving last meal requests in 2011, so Vasquez received the same meal as the other inmates: Salisbury steak, steamed rice, brown gravy, veggies, sweet peas, ranch-style beans, sliced bread, and butterscotch brownies with a choice of water, tea, or punch to drink.

BUTTERSCOTCH BROWNIES

These are lighter than your usual brownies, made with creamy butterscotch chips. They're perfect with a tall glass of milk.

MAKES: 24 brownies | **PREP TIME:** 10 minutes | **COOK TIME:** 30 minutes

INGREDIENTS

2½ cups all-purpose flour

1 teaspoon baking powder

½ teaspoon salt

1 cup (2 sticks) unsalted butter, softened

1 cup packed brown sugar

½ cup granulated sugar

1½ teaspoons vanilla extract

2 large eggs

1½ cups butterscotch chips

1. Preheat the oven to 350°F.

2. Stir the flour, baking powder and salt together in a medium bowl.

3. Using a stand mixer or a handheld mixer, beat together the butter, brown sugar, granulated sugar, and vanilla in a large bowl until smooth. Beat in the eggs one at a time. Slowly beat in the flour mixture a ½ cup at a time. Stir in the butterscotch chips.

4. Spread into an ungreased 9 x 13-inch baking pan. The batter will be thick.

5. Bake for 30 to 35 minutes, until top is a caramel brown color. Remove from the oven and cool.

HOMEMADE FRUIT PUNCH

Making your own fruit punch is pretty fun. Not only can you pretend like you're a mad scientist mixing liquids together, you can also add alcohol of your choice, which results in a delicious cocktail pitcher.

MAKES: 5 quarts | **PREP TIME:** 10 minutes

INGREDIENTS

6 cups cranberry juice

4 cups pineapple juice

4 cups orange juice

¼ cup fresh lime juice

1 liter of white lemon lime soda

lemon, lime, and orange slices

Mix all juices together in a large container. Before serving, add the soda and sliced citrus.

COY WAYNE WESBROOK

February 1, 1958–March 9, 2016

Coy Wayne Wesbrook was an American mass murderer from Texas who shot and killed five people, including his ex-wife, after discovering his ex and two men engaged in a threesome. Wesbrook's trial and conviction where not without controversy because the defense argued that his IQ was too low to understand his actions. However, the jury didn't agree, and he was executed by lethal injection in 2016.

LAST MEAL: On the day of his execution, Wesbrook was offered the prison meal (Texas no longer allowed last meal requests), which he didn't eat: baked chicken, mashed potatoes, gravy, green beans, sliced bread, and mandarin orange cake with a choice of water, tea, or punch to drink.

BUTTERY GARLIC GREEN BEANS

This is a quick and easy recipe for green beans, with butter and seasoning that enhance the flavor of the beans.

MAKES: 6 servings | **PREP TIME:** 2 minutes | **COOK TIME:** 8 minutes

INGREDIENTS

1 pound fresh green beans, ends trimmed

3 tablespoons salted butter

2 tablespoons minced fresh garlic

½ teaspoon salt

½ teaspoon black pepper

1. Place green beans into a pot and cover with water. Bring water to a simmer and cook until beans start to soften, about 5 minutes. Drain water. Add butter and garlic to green beans and cook for 3-4 minutes.

2. Season with salt and pepper. Serve warm.

HERB-BAKED CHICKEN QUARTERS

A generous seasoning of salt, pepper, and herbs is what will consistently set a flavorful moist chicken apart from dry flavorless chicken. Never skip the seasoning!

MAKES: 4 chicken quarters (serves 2 to 4) | **PREP TIME:** 10 minutes | **COOK TIME:** 40 minutes

INGREDIENTS

4 leg-thigh chicken quarters (bone in, skin on)

5 tablespoons salted butter, at room temperature

1 teaspoon salt

½ teaspoon pepper

½ tablespoon parsley flakes

¼ teaspoon ground sage

¼ teaspoon dried thyme

1. Preheat the oven to 300°F. Line a baking sheet with foil and place an oven-safe rack on the baking sheet. If you do not have a cooling rack, skip it.

2. Stir the butter, salt, pepper, parsley, sage, and thyme together in a small bowl.

3. Rub the butter into the chicken. Rub it under the skin, on top, and on both sides.

Place the chicken on the rack over the baking sheet.

4. Bake for 25 minutes, then increase the oven temperature to 425°F. Bake for about 15 minutes more. The internal temperature should be 165°F and taken in the thickest part of the meat, not touching the bone.

5. Remove the chicken from the oven and allow it to rest.

CREAMY MASHED POTATOES

A starchy russet potato is best for mashed potatoes. Also, always use real butter!

MAKES: 6 servings | **PREP TIME:** 10 minutes | **COOK TIME:** 10 minutes

INGREDIENTS

3 pounds russet potatoes, peeled and quartered

5 tablespoons salted butter

3 tablespoons sour cream

⅔ cup whole milk

1 teaspoon salt

1 teaspoon pepper

1. Boil the potatoes in a large pot until tender. Drain and place in a large bowl.

2. Add the butter and sour cream and mix with an electric mixer while slowly adding the milk. Season with salt and pepper.

HASTINGS ARTHUR WISE February 16, 1954–November 4, 2005

Hastings Arthur Wise was an American mass murderer. After being fired from his factory job, Wise opened fire on his former coworkers, killing four people. He attempted suicide by swallowing insecticide after he was done shooting, but survived to stand trial for his crimes.

Wise refused to be part of any appeals (which classified him as "voluntary" for an execution) and he was executed by lethal injection in 2005 in South Carolina.

LAST MEAL REQUEST: lobster tail, French fries, coleslaw, banana pudding, and milk.

INDIVIDUAL BANANA PUDDINGS

This recipe for a Southern classic uses fresh bananas, vanilla wafers, and banana cream pudding to bring nostalgia to any Southerner or banana lover! Enjoy as a quick and easy dessert, or for a more accurate and complete feast, serve with Coleslaw (page 36) and Homemade French Fries (page 83).

MAKES: 1 serving | **PREP TIME:** 5 minutes

6 vanilla wafers

½ cup prepared banana-flavored pudding

1 sliced banana

prepared whipped cream

Place the vanilla wafers in a circle on a place with one in the middle. Top with sliced banana and follow with the pudding. Top with whipped cream and more sliced banana. This can also be prepared in a bowl and refrigerated to let the layers meld together before serving.

BOBBY WAYNE WOODS — October 11, 1965–December 3, 2009

Bobby Wayne Woods was an American child murderer, kidnapper, and rapist. Woods's execution was delayed for a short time due to an appeal based on his low IQ (around 70) and cognitive abilities. Still, Woods ended up admitting to his crimes and the appeal ultimately failed. He was executed by lethal injection in Texas in 2009 after a gluttonous last meal.

LAST MEAL: two chicken-fried steaks; two fried chicken breasts; three fried pork chops; two hamburgers with lettuce, tomato, onion, and salad dressing; four slices of bread; half a pound of fried potatoes with onions; half a pound of onion rings with ketchup, half a pan of chocolate cake with icing; and two pitchers of milk.

CHOCOLATE LAYER CAKE

This is a great cake recipe: chocolaty, moist, and rich. You will definitely want to go in for a second slice. And a third!

MAKES: 8 servings | **PREP TIME:** 35 minutes | **COOK TIME:** 20 minutes

FOR THE CAKE:

2 cups granulated sugar

1¾ cups all-purpose flour

⅔ cup unsweetened cocoa powder

1½ teaspoons baking powder

1 teaspoon baking soda

½ teaspoon salt

2 large eggs

1 cup whole milk, at room temperature

½ cup vegetable oil

1 teaspoon vanilla extract

1 cup hot whole milk

FOR THE FILLING:

1½ cups whipped cream

2 teaspoons unsweetened cocoa powder

FOR THE CHOCOLATE BUTTERCREAM:

6 tablespoons (¾ stick) unsalted butter, softened

1¼ cups confectioner's sugar

5 ounces semisweet chocolate, melted and cooled to room temperature

¼ teaspoon vanilla extract

1½ tablespoons whole milk

1. To make the cake, preheat the oven to 350°F. Grease three 9-inch cake pans (or use just two pans for thicker layers) with butter or baking spray.

2. In a large bowl, stir together the sugar, flour, cocoa, baking powder, baking soda, and salt.

3. Add the eggs, room-temperature milk, oil, and vanilla, and stir to combine. Stir in the hot milk. Pour evenly into the prepared pans.

4. Bake for about 20 minutes, until the cake is set and does not jiggle in the middle. Cool in the pans for 10 minutes, then remove to cool completely before filling and frosting.

5. To make the filling, place the whipped cream in a medium bowl. Stir the in cocoa powder. Cover and refrigerate until ready to use.

6. To make the chocolate buttercream, combine the butter and confectioners' sugar in a stand mixer with the whisk attachment at medium-high speed. Mix in the chocolate and vanilla extract and beat until smooth; increase the speed to high if needed to help the frosting get fluffier. Add the milk ½ tablespoon at a time, blending well after each addition, until it reaches a spreadable consistency. If needed, slowly add more milk.

7. To assemble, place one layer of the cake on a plate. Spread half the filling on top, then add a second layer and spread with the remaining filling. Place the third layer on the cake. Evenly spread the buttercream over the entire cake. Slice and serve.

PHILIP WORKMAN ⟶ June 1, 1953–May 9, 2007

Philip Workman was convicted of murdering a police officer during a robbery at a Wendy's restaurant in Tennessee. Workman had previously done time for burglary and also had a serious cocaine habit. He robbed Wendy's after his first incarceration and shot Lieutenant Ronald Oliver after he arrived on the scene. There was a lot of controversy surrounding Workman's conviction because the key witness recanted his testimony that claimed he saw Workman shoot Lieutenant Oliver. This witness said he was threatened into maintaining his lies and had initially called in the false lead on Workman to collect the reward money. Furthermore, ballistic evidence indicated that the bullet most likely did not come from Workman's gun.

The execution was stayed for a time, but in 2007, the U.S. Court of Appeals for the Sixth Circuit determined that Workman had not met his burden of proof. He was executed by lethal injection that year.

LAST MEAL: Workman requested that, in lieu of a meal for himself, a large vegetarian pizza be delivered to a homeless person. The state would not honor the request, but citizens across the country sent numerous vegetarian pizzas to homeless shelters in Workman's name.

VEGGIE PIZZA

This is a quick, weeknight-friendly vegetarian pizza. It's loaded with must-haves: mushrooms, peppers, red onion, tomatoes, black olives, and spinach.

MAKES: 3 or 4 servings | **PREP TIME:** 15 minutes | **COOK TIME:** 30 minutes

INGREDIENTS

Ready-to-use refrigerated pizza dough

⅔ cup prepared pizza sauce

1¾ cup shredded mozzarella cheese

½ green bell pepper, chopped

⅛ cup sliced red onion

⅓ cup halved black olives

1 cup fresh spinach

¼ cup chopped tomatoes

⅔ cup sliced mushrooms

1. Preheat the oven to 400°F. Grease a 12-inch pizza pan with a little olive oil. Place the dough in the pan and push toward the sides to make a circle. Fold about an inch of the edge of the crust over toward the center.

2. Spread the sauce over the crust. Sprinkle the cheese evenly over the sauce.

3. Add the peppers, onion, olives, spinach, tomatoes, and mushrooms on top of the cheese.

4. Bake the pizza for 30 minutes, until the crust is golden brown and the cheese is bubbly.

HOMEMADE PIZZA DOUGH OPTION

INGREDIENTS

1 (.25-ounce) package active dry yeast

1 cup warm water

1 cup all-purpose flour

1 cup bread flour

1½ teaspoons granulated sugar

1 teaspoon salt

2 tablespoons olive oil

1. Dissolve the yeast in warm water (about 110°F). Let stand until it begins to form a creamy foam, about 5 minutes.

2. Whisk together the all-purpose flour, bread flour, sugar, and salt in the bowl of a stand mixer. Add the olive oil and yeast mixture. Mix on low speed using the dough hook until the dough sticks together and pulls away from sides. Increase the speed to medium and let it knead for 8 minutes.

3. Flour the surface of your counter. Form the dough into a round shape. Roll the dough out into a pizza crust shape.

ERIC WRINKLES ✦ January 3, 1960–December 11, 2009

Eric Wrinkles was an American mass murderer from Indiana. Wrinkles killed his ex-wife and two others in their home in 1994 and was convicted of the crime in 1995. Just weeks before the murder, Wrinkles' mother, who was worried about his erratic behavior, tried to have him institutionalized. He was deemed not disabled enough to be held at the facility and was discharged.

Prior to his execution, Wrinkles participated, via remote feed from prison, on the *Oprah Winfrey Show* and was confronted by members of the victims' family. He was executed in Indiana a few weeks later in 2009, and as of 2019, remains the last person to be executed in the state. Indiana served Wrinkles' meal three days prior to the execution because death row inmates tend to lose their appetite.

LAST MEAL: prime rib, a loaded baked potato, pork chops, steak fries, rolls, and two salads with ranch dressing.

THICK PAN-SEARED PORK CHOPS

Marinating is one of the best ways to keep pork tender. Proper seasoning and avoiding overcooking is important! Pork does not need to be cooked as well done as people used to think.

MAKES: 4 servings | **PREP TIME:** 5 minutes | **COOK TIME:** 12 minutes

INGREDIENTS

4 thick-cut pork chops (about 1½ to 2 inches thick)

1 teaspoon salt

1½ teaspoons black pepper

1 teaspoon paprika

1 teaspoon garlic powder

3 tablespoons oil

1. Mix all seasoning together in a small bowl.

2. Season the pork chops on both sides with the seasoning.

3. Heat oil in a heavy-bottomed skillet over medium heat. Place pork chops in the skillet and cook for about 5 to 6 minutes. Flip the pork chops and cook for an additional 5 minutes. Use a meat thermometer to check to see if the pork chops have reached an internal temperature of 145°F (medium-rare) to 165°F (well done), depending on your preferences.

4. Remove from the pan and allow the pork to rest for about 2 minutes, and serve.

HEARTY MIXED GREENS CHOPPED SALAD

You may have noticed that this book is full of yummy, fried, unhealthy goodness. Well, here it is: the one and only salad recipe! This one is overflowing with delicious toppings, so it's anything but boring.

MAKES: 8 Servings | **PREP TIME:** 15 minutes

INGREDIENTS

1 head of romaine

½ head of radicchio

5 cups fresh spinach

2 cup fresh arugula

½ red onion, chopped

½ cucumber, chopped

⅔ cup halved cherry tomatoes

1 cup chopped fresh broccoli

½ cups chopped fresh green beans

¼ cup sliced green onions

½ cup chopped red pepper

6 slices of cooked crispy bacon, chopped

½ cup shredded Parmesan cheese

Chop romaine, radicchio, spinach, and arugula. Combine in a large bowl with remaining ingredients. Toss to mix evenly. Serve with Homemade Buttermilk Ranch Dressing (page 111).

HOMEMADE BUTTERMILK RANCH DRESSING

There is no better dressing than ranch. And when you make your own at home, you can tweak the ingredients to make it as tangy and flavorful as you like.

MAKES: 1¼ cups | **PREP TIME:** 5 minutes | **REST TIME:** 4 hours

INGREDIENTS

- ⅓ cup mayonnaise
- ½ cup sour cream
- ½ cup buttermilk
- 1 tablespoon dried parsley
- 1 teaspoon dried dill

- ½ teaspoon apple cider vinegar
- ½ teaspoon garlic powder
- ¼ teaspoon onion powder
- ¼ teaspoon salt
- ¼ teaspoon black pepper

Whisk together mayo, sour cream, and buttermilk. Add remaining ingredients and stir. Cover and allow it to rest in the fridge for 4 hours.

AILEEN WUORNOS — February 29, 1956–October 9, 2002

Aileen Wuornos may have lived in the Sunshine State, but she was no ray of light. In fact, she was one of America's most well-known serial killers. Wuornos had a hard childhood filled with abuse. After giving birth to a child, Wuornos dropped out of school at age 14. Wuornos's abusive grandfather kicked her out when she was 15, and she took to living in the woods near her old home. Soon she was engaged in petty crimes and prostitution.

Wuornos was responsible for the execution-style murders of seven men in 1989 and 1990. She claimed all of her victims had attacked and assaulted her, and that she killed in self-defense. Despite her testimony, she was convicted of six murders and sentenced to die by lethal injection, making her the tenth woman in the United States and second in Florida to be executed.

LAST MEAL: Wuornos declined her meal and had a hamburger and a few snacks from the canteen and coffee later in the day.

HAMBURGERS

Feel free to add your favorite toppings, like lettuce, tomato, onion, cheese, and even bacon (see Oven-Baked Bacon, page 69).

MAKES: 4 hamburgers | **PREP TIME:** 10 minutes | **COOK TIME:** 10 minutes

INGREDIENTS

1¼ pounds ground beef (80/20 fat ratio)

½ teaspoon salt

½ teaspoon pepper

¼ teaspoon seasoned salt

¼ teaspoon garlic powder

¼ teaspoon onion powder

1 tablespoon melted butter

4 hamburger buns

1. Mix the salt, pepper, seasoned salt, garlic powder, and onion powder together in a small dish. Place the ground beef in a large bowl and add the seasonings.

2. Using your hands, gently combine the meat and seasonings. Pat into 4 equal-sized round patties.

3. Heat a grill to medium high. Grill the burgers for 4 minutes and then flip. Use a meat thermometer to ensure that the burgers reach your desired temperature, or about 160°F. Remove the burgers from the grill and cover to keep warm.

4. Brush the insides of the buns with melted butter and place on the grill to lightly toast. Remove and serve the burgers on the with the toasted buns, with toppings as desired.

SERVE WITH: Homemade French Fries (page 83) and Strawberry Milkshakes (page 82) for a full diner-style spread.

CONCLUSION

Well, that's the end of the line for us. I'm striving not to leave a bad taste in your mouth, but still tastefully tantalize your brain and taste buds with truly heinous crimes and delicious recipes inspired by the killers' final days. Fancy a spooky dinner party? Need a few grisly appetizers for a watch party of your favorite scary show? Or maybe a sweet treat for movie night? Whatever poison you pick, thank you for letting me share my love of true crime and food with you.

CONVERSIONS

Volume

U.S.	U.S. Equivalent	Metric
1 tablespoon (3 teaspoons)	½ fluid ounce	15 milliliters
¼ cup	2 fluid ounces	60 milliliters
⅓ cup	3 fluid ounces	90 milliliters
½ cup	4 fluid ounces	120 milliliters
⅔ cup	5 fluid ounces	150 milliliters
¾ cup	6 fluid ounces	180 milliliters
1 cup	8 fluid ounces	240 milliliters
2 cups	16 fluid ounces	480 milliliters

Weight

U.S.	Metric
½ ounce	15 grams
1 ounce	30 grams
2 ounces	60 grams
¼ pound	115 grams
⅓ pound	150 grams
½ pound	225 grams
¾ pound	350 grams
1 pound	450 grams

THE SERIAL KILLER COOKBOOK

Temperature

Fahrenheit (°F)	Celsius (°C)
100°F	40°C
120°F	50°C
130°F	55°C
140°F	60°C
150°F	65°C
160°F	70°C
170°F	75°C
180°F	80°C
190°F	90°C
200°F	95°C
220°F	105°C
240°F	115°C
260°F	125°C
280°F	140°C
300°F	150°C
325°F	165°C
350°F	175°C
375°F	190°C
400°F	200°C
425°F	220°C

RECIPE INDEX

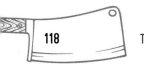

ACKNOWLEDGMENTS

I want to thank my family for supporting me, my ideas, and my interests that take me off the beaten path. To my husband, Ron; my parents, Sara and Mike; my sister, Rachel; and my nephew, Gabe: Thank you for being as excited as I am! To my kids, Kellen and Rowan, thanks for being completely oblivious to what your mother was working on because you are far too young to read this book, but I look forward to the day I can show you. Thanks for being my Why. To my Lecker father, mother, sister, and brother, thank you for supporting me and showing curiosity about this wild ride.

To my friends, there are so many of you to thank for your interest, support, love, and ability to keep from running when I talked about case details and research for this book—I appreciate it all. Amanda (my murderino), Emily, Elena, Rachel (my lovely sister), Maggie, Bridget, Sara, and Melissa: You are amazing, and I am so honored to have you with me while I worked on this project. Thank you for always being my outlets and for listening to me.

To my Cheese Curd in Paradise readers: I am so happy that I can finally share this with you because so much of my passion comes from my readers. To all my twisted true crime-loving crew, this was a thrill, and I hope you love it as much as I do.

Finally, I'd like to thank Ulysses Press, especially Claire Sielaff, for supporting me, answering all my questions, and bringing this obscure niche to the masses with me.

ABOUT THE AUTHOR

Ashley Lecker is a true crime lover, avid recipe developer, barre devotee, and general history nerd. Ashley is a graduate of Edgewood College in Madison, Wisconsin, and the University of Wisconsin-Green Bay. She previously worked in the public sector for the House of Representatives and at a nonprofit before obtaining her teaching license. Ashley currently works in her local school system, and develops and publishes her blog, *Cheese Curd in Paradise*. Ashley lives in Green Bay, Wisconsin, with her husband, two sons, and her cats. She enjoys traveling with her family, watching the Green Bay Packers, and enjoying a cold beer on her patio.

THE SERIAL KILLER COOKBOOK